Helping

Your Grandchildren

Through Their Parents'

Divorce

Helping

Your Grandchildren

Through Their Parents'

Divorce

JOAN SCHRAGER COHEN

WALKER AND COMPANY
NEW YORK

First published in the United States of America in 1994 by Walker
Publishing Company, Inc.

Published simultaneously in Canada by Thomas Allen & Son Canada,
Limited, Markham, Ontario

Library of Congress Cataloging-in-Publication Data
Cohen, Joan Schrager.
Helping your grandchildren through their parents' divorce / Joan
Schrager Cohen.
p.   cm.
Includes bibliographical references (p.   ) and index.
ISBN 0-8027-1298-3. —ISBN 0-8027-7433-4 (pbk.)
1. Children of divorced parents—Family relationships.
2. Grandparent and child—Family relationships.
3. Intergenerational relations.   4. Divorced people—Family
relationships.   I. Title.
HQ777.6.C62   1994
306.874'5—dc20   94-9986
CIP

Book design by Claire Naylon Vaccaro

Printed in the United States of America

2   4   6   8   10   9   7   5   3   1

To
Alyson, Emilee, and Zachary
who have taught me (and are still teaching me)
the art of grandparenting from A to Z.

Contents

&

Acknowledgments

§

If it weren't for the grandparents, parents, and grandchildren who shared their stories and emotions with me, this book would not have been written. To all of them, I extend my gratitude.

Thanks to Bob, a patient husband, who endured my writing in cars, buses, and planes, in restaurants (on the backs of place mats), and just about anywhere we happened to be when a thought would occur.

To Patricia A. Tipton, a typist extraordinaire—a very special thank you.

Christopher Eli Kraus deserves recognition, not only for being a fine son-in-law but because he urged me on when I was in the throes of self-doubt.

Sally Brush, director of Beech Acres' Aring Institute in Cincinnati, Ohio, understands the role played by today's grandparents. My thanks to her for imparting this wisdom to me.

I am truly indebted to Marc Rabinowitz, of Psychotherapy Associates of Ghent, Ltd. in Norfolk, Virginia. He explained to me the psychological underpinnings of grandchildren who must live through their parents' divorce, and made me aware of the needs of single parents and grandparents as well.

My deep appreciation goes to a number of experts in the legal and behavioral science fields who gave me insight into the complex nature of the grandparent-grandchild relationship when there is only one active parent in the family. In the legal field: Judge Joanne F. Alper, Arlington Juvenile and Domestic Relations District Court, Arlington, Virginia; Judge Frederick P. Aucamp (retired), Virginia Beach, Virginia; Roslyn Brown, attorney at Howell, Daugherty, Brown, and Lawrence, Norfolk, Virginia; Mary G. Commander, attorney, Norfolk, Virginia; Tazewell T. Hubard III, attorney and mediator, Norfolk, Virginia; Judge Lawrence L. Koontz, Jr., Court of Appeals of Virginia, Salem, Virginia; Dr. Ken Lewis, director of Child Custody Services, Philadelphia, Pennsylvania; Paul M. Lipkin, attorney, Norfolk, Virginia; and William B. Smith, attorney and commissioner in the chancery of the Virginia Beach Circuit Court, Virginia Beach, Virginia. In the behavioral science field: Jennette M. Franklin, social worker, Norfolk, Virginia; Jane Kaminski, health educator, Virginia Beach, Virginia; Gayle M. Mallinger, former supervisor of Clinical Services at Jewish Family Services of Tidewater, Norfolk, Virginia; Dr. Charles E. Parker, child and adult psychiatrist, Virginia Beach, Virginia; and Bonnie Winters, divorce program specialist at Beech Acres' Aring Institute, Cincinnati, Ohio.

I appreciate the assistance of Stanwood Dickman, an accountant in Virginia Beach, Virginia, in providing financial advice for grandparents.

Dr. Karen Lewis is a friend, author, and family therapist. Her encouragement in the early days of this endeavor meant so much to me.

Acknowledgments

Aly and Zach are my own grandchildren of divorce. I thank them both for painstakingly and lovingly guiding me into *living* this book, rather than just writing it.

Lastly, I am beholden to my own grandparents, Esther Cohen and Samuel Schrager, of blessed memory. They knew the true meaning of being a GRANDparent.

Helping

Your Grandchildren

Through Their Parents'

Divorce

§

Introduction

§

It didn't seem like such a difficult task at the time . . . to find a survival manual or a primer on how to help our grandchildren through their parents' divorce. What my husband and I were looking for was a plan of action, some stated goals, a few proven attitudes and behaviors that we could adopt or adapt. Unfortunately for us, the few books to be found in our nearby library and the local bookstore left too many gaps. They did not give us the means to handle our pain and that of our grandchildren.

To the core of our being, we could sense the anguish of our grandchildren. Dr. Arthur Kornhaber, founder and president of the Foundation for Grandparenting and the author of *Grandparents/Grandchildren: The Vital Connection*, confirms in his research (as do other studies) that "children of divorce experience rejection and feelings of abandonment, to which they react with anger, fear, guilt, insecurity, and resentment." Dr. Kornhaber further sensitized us to the concern that our grandchildren would devalue adults in general and sustain other emotional scars. Would they grow up to mistrust the very institution of marriage?

We were searching for words we could say and actions we could take that might somehow empower our changing family. We needed to be a source of strength for our daughter, who was facing the trials and tribulations of single parenthood. A fallout occurs when an intact family suddenly becomes disenfranchised owing to the absence of one parent. And if the noncustodial parent is disengaged, a continual cloud is cast. There is derision; there is a chasm and, often, righteous indignation on the part of the custodial parent and the grandchildren. Single mothers or fathers are heroic in many ways, large and small. They try to make up to their children for the absent, negligent, or destructive parent.

In their book *Grandparenting for the Nineties*, Doctors Robert A. Aldrich and Glenn Austin evaluate the stresses of single parenthood. They make mention of the obvious opportunity that exists here for grandparents to parent their single adult child, who, "almost above all, needs love and support so that he or she can pass it on to the children—YOUR GRANDCHILDREN" (p. 144). Moreover, Aldrich and Austin make the point that it is an unenviable task for these single parents to offer security and love to their children when they are not receiving any themselves.

When our family discovered the lack of reading material, I began to look for other grandparents who might have experienced such a crisis or were presently living through the chaos of a divorcing child and its aftermath. I wound up interviewing more than sixty-seven grandparents (plus scores of parents, grandchildren, and experts in the legal and behavioral science fields), whose words of wisdom are scattered through this book. Although each grandparent's experience is special in its singularity, there is a common theme here: grandparents worry about the vulnerability of their grandchildren. Those who are distanced geographically seem the most distressed. (Alas, my husband and I fell into that category.) Yet by practicing creative grandparenting and reaching out to the youngest generation, many of these long-distance grandparents showed us how much can be accomplished when the will, the conviction, and the commitment are present.

There are roadblocks, to be sure, but in each case I found that grandparents are indeed making a difference in the lives of their grandchildren. The philosophy of Beech Acres' Aring Institute, Cincinnati, Ohio, a well-respected divorce clinic, is that "a patient, nurturing grandparent can reduce the emotional impact of divorce for many a grandchild." As one grandparent succinctly put it, "When their parents divorce, the children lose their center."

Social scientists have frequently stated that the attention, respect, and concern that grandparents exhibit toward their grandchildren can enhance the grandchildren's self-image.

Grandparents are accustomed to the variables and injustices of life. They have learned to cope with adversity and know all about the fragility of life. Building on cumulative life experiences, they can, as the true "grown-ups" in this unfolding drama, become teachers or role models to their grandchildren (and children). During the various stages of divorce, grandchildren are desperately seeking mentors. Grandparents can help build their grandchildren's confidence and competency. More important, they can offer them a positive outlook on life.

When I interviewed a cross-section of grandchildren for this book, many boasted of having more than one grandparent, and those who were part of merged families, sometimes acquiring four sets of grandparents, said they were the envy of their peers!

Dr. Arthur Kornhaber, founder and president of the Foundation for Grandparenting, asserts in *Grandparents/Grandchildren: The Vital Connection* that "if grandparents did not exist, children would surely invent them" (p. 48). The need by children for intimacy and continuity of family has been with us for centuries. "Grandparents tend to underestimate their importance to their grandchildren" add Drs. Aldrich and Austin (p. 227). "Simply knowing that they have or had grandparents means more to children than most think," they claim.

Grandchildren need the wisdom that grandparents can impart; grandparents can reap the rewards of being mentors and family historians. Grandchildren learn from the achievements of the grandparents, and even from some of their self-professed errors! If grandparents offer a model of maturity, compassion, and experience, they can be imitated. Another plus is that grandparents can challenge each grandchild to live up to his or her potential.

Our increasingly mobile society often separates the generations. Many children have no way of knowing their extended family. Yet beleaguered families cry out for a sense of belonging and familial roots—of "connectedness." Family history gives a child a sense of belonging. "To have roots," says Dr. Kornhaber, "is to know where you come from and therefore who you are" (p. 169). As the guardian of the family history and heritage, along with being the official biographer of grandchildren's parents, the grandparent is a storehouse of valuable information. Children delight in hearing stories about when their parents were young, especially those about pranks and foibles. It confirms to them that their parents were once children, too—and not perfect, either. Children's natural curiosity extends to their family roots. They will continually seek out their identity and try to figure out who they are, where they belong in the family's hierarchy, and how they are similar to, yet different from, other family members. An interested grandparent can guide a child through the tangled web of family history with photo albums, scrapbooks, and special grandparent stories—which then become part of the child's own life story.

"A child's image of old age and therefore his own 'ending' is shaped to a large degree by the presence or absence of at least one close grandparent," says Dr. Kornhaber (p. 110). This view is shared by the psychologists, psychiatrists, and family therapists I interviewed in the course of writing this book.

According to many of the same experts, grandparents are often viewed by their grandchildren as being closer to God because of their age and therefore can better communicate and are more believable when espousing values and religion to their grandchildren.

An interesting observation by Drs. Aldrich and Austin is that "children need content and happy grandparents to emulate who have retained a sense of humor" (p. 227). Enjoying grandparenting cannot be faked, for children are almost clairvoyant at seeing through phonies! When this "enjoyment of grandparenting" is genuine, grandchildren come to the conclusion that raising kids can be fun, albeit hard work, and that sacrifices should be made for the good of the family. They can witness firsthand a style of parenting that dispenses with complaints and self-pity, so they get the idea that parenting is rewarding. (Even though this may be parenting once removed.) The positive message is both subtle and overt: "These people care about me, they act upon their caring, they do their job, and sometimes they even have fun doing it!"

The grandparents with whom I talked were especially distraught about the emotional insecurity of their grandchildren, wrought by the fragmentation of the divorce. They shared with me a gamut of emotions ranging from disillusionment and depression to indignation, resentment, and helplessness. But grandparents who were positive thinkers and those who could develop a plan of action were able to leave behind precarious inclinations, transcending their pain and inertia, and move toward resolve, resiliency, and eventual recovery. Their own recovery significantly enhanced that of the new family.

Unfortunately, some grandparents write off their grandchildren along with their children's failed marriage. Research indicates that there appears to be a disconnection from their grandchildren by some grandparents when what is genuinely needed for the divided family is *more connection to family.*

The reluctance to grandparent sometimes arises because of the association that grandparenthood has with being old. There are those who try to avoid active grandparenting because they simply have no memory of exposure to their own grandparents and have trouble feeling comfortable in the role. It is often difficult for disconnected grandparents to even admit that their grandchildren might possibly need them or that they, the grandparents, can do anything constructive to strengthen the family. Other reasons given for noninvolvement include "I don't want to interfere," and "I'm not sure what I could do to help" (equating help with money, rather than with hands-on gifts of time or sharing).

Grandparenthood is a forgotten source of family strength, a much underestimated reservoir. As one grandmother expressed to me, "There is no substitute for family. Our grandchildren can be impoverished without necessarily being poor. It is the souls of our grandchildren that will remain impoverished unless we, acting as the 'family preservationists,' reclaim our power."

As I began to hear and document the grandparent stories and those of many grandchildren and parents, I soon realized that there were many other dimensions to this new journey between grandchild and grandparent. There were issues I had not been aware of. To begin with, many grandparents are uncertain of their rights with respect to grandchildren who have been separated from them by divorce or remarriage. They find themselves wading through the legal complexities of grandparent visitation and custody. Some grandparents, unjustly denied visitation with their grandchildren, are waging court battles to regain these rights. Others are resigned to having no contact with their grandchildren either because they lack the funds to fight their case and/or because they delude themselves into thinking that "there's nothing we can do."

When a grandparent escalates hostilities with "the other side," or when disparaging remarks, attitude, and behavior about the custodial parent (or, for that matter, either parent) are taken to extremes, the courts may disallow grandparental visitation. Psychologists and court personnel wrestle with this aspect of divorce continually. In addition to the possible curtailment of visitation with a grandchild, the grandparent who acts in such a fashion risks aiding and abetting the grandchild's instability.

Dotted along the pathways of interviews and research, I encountered social scientists expressing their concern about philosophical differences in parenting between the generations. A lack of understanding or respect for these differences can cause added conflicts, thus creating more insecurity for the grandchildren.

Shall we remain on a collision course at the expense of our grandchildren? Just as in a war zone, children are the ones caught in the cross fire—innocent victims of the warring parties. It is not just the divorcing parents but often the parents and the grandparents who do battle, to the detriment of all.

Grandparents who may have been or who are now estranged from their son or daughter would do well to see this crisis as an opportunity to re-create or renew a previously failed relationship. Should wounded pride stand in the way of building family cohesiveness for grandchildren who so badly need a strong family unit? Perhaps out of this adversity will come a second chance for harmonious relations.

Trying to establish a healthy relationship with the grandchild's parent(s), especially when it is the grandparent's own son or daughter who has custody, is of paramount importance to a grandchild's stability. Bad feelings can often cause a grandchild additional pain, over and above what he or she is already experiencing from the divorce. Grandparent and adult child, as well as the other side, may need professional help to achieve the harmony necessary for the well-being of the grandchildren.

There is a deep alienation in our society between parents and grandparents, and the losers are the grandchildren. The generational gap and philosophical difference of values, especially parenting values, must be bridged somehow.

We grandparents need to look for additional ways to become allies with the custodial parent primarily but the other parent as well. The challenge of avoiding confrontation, especially within earshot or view of the children, must be worked on and worked on and worked on until we have succeeded in establishing a relationship that is built on mutual respect.

As one family therapist notes, "The highest hurdle of all is reaching into yourself and finding new ways to impart vision, verve, and vitality to lead a troubled family. The toughest jump is not how to get along with the grandchildren; it's establishing a workable dialogue with their parents that makes the rest fall in place."

We must negotiate our differences for the benefit of the grandchildren. If this requires professional help, so be it. More and more support groups for grandparents (and the entire family) are developing across the country in hospitals, churches, synagogues, family service associations, YMCAs and YWCAs, community centers, and so on. (See chapter 4 for information on starting your own support group.)

"We are increasingly becoming an age-irrelevant society," says sociologist Bernice Neugarten. As she notes in Dr. Kornhaber's book, "the most powerful new age group lies between the ages of fifty-five and seventy. These 'young-old' are healthier, more affluent, and better educated than any group of elders before them" (p. 162). Not only are the expected ages at which people fill traditional social roles becoming scrambled, but how they choose to act in these roles varies according to the individual and his or her own comfort level. As far as grandparenting is concerned, there are a variety of styles that can be adopted. A grandpa can be a best friend ("he's my buddy"; "I take 'em out to the ball game"). A grandma can lead cultural outings (to the ballet, the symphony, a play) and/or provide cookies and milk after school. There is the teacher-mentor grandparent, the church- or synagogue-going grandparent, and so on. Caretaking is but one of numerous activities that make up the role of grandparenting today.

Whatever your "grandparent perspective" may be, the social workers, family therapists, and psychologists are in full accord about grandparents *not* becoming martyrs for their children and/or grandchildren. There are ways to maintain our dreams and pursuits, careers, and other familial relationships while still helping to build a more secure foundation for those whose wounds we wish to bind. It is indeed a learning process for all three generations. The positive assessment from the experts is that this is all "teachable" if one has an open mind and is receptive to change.

I decided to write this book when I realized that my husband and I were actually "living the book." In fact, it has taken me longer than planned to gather my thoughts, research, and interviews and place them on paper, simply because I have wanted to take time out to grandparent our grandchildren in the various stages of accommodation to their new way of life.

My husband, daughter, grandchildren, and myself have now lived and experienced all of these stages. First came the devastating news of the breakup of the marriage of our daughter and the loss of the relationship we had once shared with a beloved young couple. Second, when our grandchildren's other parent moved out of the home, we could feel the pain. It was layered with disturbing qualities of hollowness and loss, almost as in a death. Although we lived a thousand miles away, we began an odyssey of travel, phone calls, letter writing, tape sending, packages, and continuous contact with our grieving offspring and those faraway grandchildren.

The third stage of this process came just ten months after the separation, when we found our child and grandchildren on our doorstep. They moved into our home and lived with us for four months. Three generations under one roof! We learned the hard way, by trial and error, that it is necessary to set ground rules in the early days of living together. All the love and good intentions on both sides cannot preclude setting parameters.

Many of the experts that you will meet in this book recommend drawing up a contract for all parties so that definitive duties and responsibilities are clear from the beginning. This is something we had not anticipated or fully analyzed. But now, drawing upon many interviews and from our own experience, we see the merits of such a plan. "A three-generational alliance," as it is referred to by family therapist Marc Rabinowitz, "is a necessity."

We are presently in stage four. Our child and grandchildren live in a house about ten minutes from our home. The children come here after school approximately three afternoons a week until their mother comes for them after work. In chapter 3, you will be given a host of suggestions for entertaining your grandchildren. And in chapter 4, you will read about the trials, tribulations, and adjustments involved in manning the way station!

On many weekends (or at least one day out of the weekend) we try and do things as a family. There are basketball or soccer games, cookouts, shopping expeditions, sleepovers, picnics, treks to the beach, and things like teaching our young grandson to ride his bicycle without training wheels. As one very precocious grandchild whispered to me, "Grandparents sort of take the place of a mommy or daddy when they're not around!"

It has been a few years since the initial state of disarray in our grandchildren's lives. And as I write, there is still a litany of lessons to be learned. Accommodating one another's space and respecting differing generational viewpoints are what we are currently working on. (And if and when our daughter remarries, we will be confronted with stage five: new beginnings, perhaps stepgrandchildren, and other accommodations to be made.)

Our grandchildren are well on their way to adjusting to their new environs (a new city, a new home, a new school, a new neighborhood, and new friends). We can sense their new calmness. They don't wake up with nightmares, as they once did. They smile and laugh a lot now—and tell jokes. Hugs are high on everyone's agenda!

No, we cannot take the place of their missing parent. And there are emotional scars and some regression from time to time. But by and large, we see healthy, happy, growing children. We have thrown them an anchor, so to speak, that they may better navigate a storm-filled sea. And we see before our eyes the results of our "rescue mission." Our grandchildren are developing an awareness of the *nature of family*, along with renewed self-esteem. They have, we hope, arrived at a threshold from which to grow into mature, caring human beings. We cannot make everything perfect, as we explain, but we can help to guide them through the abyss. Our goal is to strengthen their self-worth as we help them seek a sense of belonging to a larger entity that requires work and sacrifice for the good of all.

Grandchildren living in the throes of divided families need mentors and "mensches." "Mensch" is of Yiddish derivation and means "a person of integrity and honor." A mensch looks at the long view of life rather than simply the short haul. He or she rises above the fray and the pettiness of family bickering for the welfare of the grandchildren and the family as a whole. (Perhaps a mensch would build bridges to the other side no matter who is at fault and would help keep open the lines of communication to the absent or estranged parent.)

The rise in single-parent households, usually those with working single parents, will only grow in numbers, says author Sam Keen in his book *Fire in the Belly*. Keen states that in the next two decades, one out of every five children will live in a household without a father. (Grandfathers have an unparalleled opportunity and the ability to redress the pervasive lack of male influence in the lives of their grandchildren!)

Grandparenthood transcends race, religion, socioeconomic distinctions, class, and culture. Wherever I looked, I found grandparents who were active, vital people. Because of the economic downturn and back-to-back recessions of the last decade, many grandparents still find it necessary to remain in the workplace. And then again, many work because they want to. Grandparents also make up the bulk of volunteerism.

Grandmothers work, run a home, cook, get their hair coiffed— and still find time to play with, love, and occasionally care for their grandchildren.

Grandfathers work, watch sports on TV, travel, take their grandchildren to baseball games, count the strands on top of their head, and wish their son or daughter wasn't a single parent.

So here, then, is the dichotomy, the heart of the debate: How can we find a balance—be a part of our grandchildren's world (especially when that world has exploded) while still maintaining our own goals, aspirations, work, hobbies, and other relationships?

Where will we place our priorities? How will we handle the ambiguities? Can we act in the best interest of our grandchildren, our own best interest, and that of our family, too? Can we grandparents be counted on to come forward and save a lost generation of children (who are our very own grandchildren)? Such are the dilemmas that this book attempts to explore.

1.
The End
and the Beginning

§

THE BREAKUP OF A CHILD'S

MARRIAGE

Unrealistic expectations. Most of us suffer from this malady. When it comes to thinking in terms of our child's marriage, we are often caught unawares. The majority of us are traditionalists: we have an expectation of family cohesiveness. This attitude persists even though 49 percent of all marriages end in divorce. But then, at times without any warning, our child divorces. His or her life appears to be shattered; our grandchildren's lives are fragmented, and their journey has changed course irrevocably.

In many tight-knit families, divorce represents a loss almost like a death. Parents of divorcing children do a tremendous amount of soul searching. Did we do something wrong? Did we interfere too much? Were we not supportive enough? Should we have seen it coming?

There are still many parents of adult children who do not believe in divorce or who do not see it coming. Many delude themselves into thinking and believing that all is well. As one parent explained, "They were just here for the weekend, and we could hear them pushing the beds together as they always do. Three days later, we get a call from our son that our daughter-in-law wants out of the marriage! Not only were we hurt and concerned for our grandchildren but we worried about our son's emotional health. We were grieving for our lost 'daughter,' too."

Emily Brown, director of a therapy and mediation center in Virginia, speaks to this issue: "Many parents never let go of the idea that they are responsible for how well their kids do, or for how poorly their kids do. And they feel that there is something the matter with their parenting if they have a kid who splits up."

Marc Rabinowitz, a family therapist in Virginia, says, "When I see parents whose children have just divorced, there is a level of concern voiced as to what their son or daughter may have learned from them as to maintaining a healthy marital relationship."

In addition to feeling somewhat responsible for the breakup of the marriage, parents of divorcing children typically experience a general feeling of malaise and disruption. Some parents speak in interviews of their feelings of humiliation and shame. Others say they carry around a sense of failure that often extends into their marital relationships, their ties with siblings and elderly parents, and their careers.

One couple expressed concern that they were becoming thin-skinned because of their deep hurt. "All of a sudden, remarks that wouldn't have raised an eyebrow felt like salt in an open wound" is how one grandfather put it. "We seemed so susceptible to hurts and slights from each other, friends, store clerks, just about anyone."

A PERIOD OF MOURNING

Grandparents Jim and Ellen discuss the period of mourning in their family:

When we discovered our daughter and son-in-law were separating and would ultimately be divorcing, we did not want to leave our home. We canceled attendance at meetings, declined invitations to dinner, gave away concert and theater tickets. We didn't even want to be with our best friends. We were "circling the wagons," pulling in, closing ranks—whatever you want to call it. We felt the need to just be with each other or alone or "alone together." Coincidentally, our daughter and her two children, who were going through the "first degree" pain of divorce and living in another state, felt the same way. Even our five-year-old grandson told his mother that he didn't want to go out to play. "Everyone is staring at me. They know!"

Jim and Ellen's story is typical in many ways. The consensus of the therapists I interviewed is that this "circling the wagons" is very normal behavior. It is a natural state of mourning. One psychologist recommends that you "don't rush it; let it wash over you like an ocean wave."

Some grandparents compare the feelings that they experience after their son or daughter's divorce to the grief process following the loss of a spouse or a parent. Understanding this may give a sense of hope that the terrible ache will heal and that one will survive.

For some individuals, this state of mourning may last only a matter of weeks. For others, it may take months. But if grieving becomes embroiled with other deep-seated problems ("old baggage," as the psychologists call it) and affects other relationships, professional help may be needed to sort out or process feelings and to find the necessary plan of action to lead to recovery. (In succeeding chapters I will give you a plan that will jump-start your healing and allow you to connect positively with your grandchildren and their parent. For grandparent support groups, see chapter 4.)

Constance Ahrons, professor of sociology at the University of Southern California, holds that "the pain a child's divorce brings [to the parent] often depends on how long the marriage has lasted and whether or not there are grandchildren." It is not simply the worry over the grandchildren's pain and loss, but more specifically the fear and uncertainty for their future, that compounds the various tiers of pain.

As one grandfather tells it: "You don't want to see your kids hurt, whether it's slipping off a diving board or in their marital life. I think that's a greater pain than bearing it yourself!" Almost without exception, moral and legal quandaries pale before that most basic of human instincts: the desire of a parent to take on and take away the pain of a child and a grandchild.

However, Dr. Charles Parker, a Virginia psychiatrist and author, notes the pitfalls of an undertaking that tries to remove *all* the pain of your divorcing child. "Five years down the road or ten or twenty or for a lifetime, your child will resent it if you try and take away or take over *all* their pain. She or he has to handle it! You can help them see the need for balance in their life. You can help them adjust. You tell them, 'Yes, this is traumatic, but you are a tough person. Terrible things do happen unfortunately to good people, but *you will get through it.*' "

Dr. Parker emphasizes the point that as parents and grandparents, we can help guide this divided family into realizing that life is constantly changing and the person(s) who can handle change will make it in this world.

He compares a weeping willow tree in a terrible storm with the straight and erect tree. The wind and the torrents of rain rarely shake the weeping willow apart or knock it down. It bends and moves with the whim of nature. Yet the straight and unbending tree, although seemingly strong, which has never been out of shape, will more than likely snap in two.

Dr. Parker's view is that as grandparents we can act as teachers and mentors: "We have the wisdom of life's experiences to realize that every crisis is an opportunity to grow and to learn if you perceive it as such. We as grandparents and parents need to get across to our child and to our grandchildren that in the best interest of each individual and the family, it is not healthy to wallow in self-pity. Empathize, yes, identify with their hurt, but teach them to survive. Adopt a positive focus and help empower your child and your grandchildren with a solidarity of purpose." He also reminds us that we, the grandparents, are accustomed to the variables and injustices of life. We've learned how to take our licks and to keep bouncing back. The grandchildren's lives and the life of our son or daughter need sound judgment and the restoration of *balance*. We have the ability to place them all in a stronger position to cope with the contingencies of life.

THE IMPORTANT ROLE OF GRANDPARENTING

While some part of your family life may be over, a new chapter is about to begin. This is when you, the grandparent, can be the most powerful tool for the new, emerging family. Children can thrive in many circumstances, but there is a hole at the center of a child's life where a father or mother once was.

Grandparents can come forward at this juncture and help to preserve the sanctity of the family. According to Dr. Arthur Korn-haber, grandparents who have a stronger sense of altruism will find this involvement far easier. He refers to the fact that much of the fabric of modern family life has unraveled due in part to an over-concern for individualism. All to often the mores of today's world weaken the bonds between grandparents and grandchildren rather than reinforce them. Dr. Kornhaber hones an important point when he suggests that we need to move past the view that strength-ening emotional ties is somehow akin to "emotional bondage."

Other psychologists agree and suggest we will have to be cre-ative and throw away the social script that has been handed down to us by the "modern" family with its safe distance between the generations.

While the original family of a grandchild struggles to cope, you can offer that grandchild a reaffirmation or a renewed faith in humanity. You can show you are indeed a person that can be counted on. A recent study supports the notion that a substantive and cooperative mother-grandmother relationship is nearly as effective as a normal mother-father family in sustaining the psychological well-being and social adaptability of children.

The same study indicates the need for grandfathers as male role models for today's children (most grandchildren are raised by women). As grandfathers contemplate establishing a meaningful relationship with their grandchildren, they may want to remember a truism which has endured for centuries: Grandchildren are a source of joy to most grandfathers.

Sometimes grandfathers put aside these feelings because of their work or because they may not be fully aware of their significance in the lives of grandchildren of divorce. Fear of being viewed as "old" (the Grandpa syndrome) may preclude some grandfathers from even attempting the role of grandfatherhood. Those who are more enlightened benefit from their involvement, as they tell in their stories.

Many grandfathers speak of shared friendship with their grandchildren and a new "bonding" that they did not even have with their own children. Others refer to the fun they have in playing with their grandchildren: "This is by far the best time in my life. We play ball, take walks, talk about everything under the sun . . . just getting into a child's mind is fascinating. I wish that I had had this insight (and time) when my own kids were growing up!" One very active grandfather says, "These are the dividends on my investment."

Gail Mallinger, a social worker for the Jewish Family Service in Norfolk, Virginia, sees the grandfather as a stand-in for Dad. "There is a perception by children that dads are for fun . . . sports, roughhousing, projects, et cetera. If possible, find a grandfather if no dad is around."

According to Marc Rabinowitz, "Boys and dads sometimes have difficulty in talking about substantive things. Thus you see roughhousing and wrestling as replacements. I notice also that where there is an absent father . . . the boys that manage to grow into adult males with the least amount of problems are the ones that somehow have made a connection to a mentor—a man."

Mallinger points out how grandfathers are also very important to little girls. "How we as women interrelate with a man and how we learn to feel good about ourselves comes from the men we are closest to early in life. If you don't have an active father around, a loving grandfather will surely help."

Divided families are an affliction of modern life. But there are many things we can do to contribute to the lives of our grandchildren. It's not necessary to be all things to all people. We can employ any number of skills or comfortable roles—from storyteller to chauffeur.

The late M. F. K. Fisher, eloquent food writer for *The New Yorker* and author of fifteen books, was often called to task for writing about such "trifles" as food. Her retort: "It seems to me that our three most basic needs: food, security, and love, are so mixed and mingled and entwined, that we cannot straightaway think of one without the others. So it happens that when I write of hunger, I am really writing about love."

Many grandparents underestimate the powerful message of love and caring that is mixed and blended into their cakes, cookies, and other culinary efforts. Just bringing good things to eat, sending "care packages" of food, or having the family to dinner or for snacks after school is a sign that you love them. And if grandparents are too busy or simply don't like to cook, picking up their favorite fried chicken or Chinese food and dropping it off, or sending their favorite dessert, sends a strong message.

Anthropologist Colleen Johnson says that in spite of the negative attitudes and tough talk by some grandparents about not wanting to be involved with their grandchildren when the parents divorce, she found that most did eventually help. This seemed to be true especially when their children and grandchildren were having "troubles." Adds Johnson, "When a divorce occurs, grandparents' actions don't usually follow their professed and somewhat hostile-sounding philosophy."

Johnson further notes that involved grandmothers define their role as "advocates" for their grandchildren; at times even mediating with the parents. "Most grandmothers," attests Johnson, "recognize the need to be there, provide love and security, stability, family, and continuity." Most of the San Francisco grandmothers that she observed gave both financial and emotional support.

(For more information on the grandparent-grandchild relationship, see chapter 3.)

LENDING ASSISTANCE IMMEDIATELY AFTER
THE BREAKUP

Children have proven to be extremely resourceful in adjusting to the exterior and interior crises in their lives. Researchers over the years have observed that the resiliency of children is superior to that of grown-ups in situations such as divorce. Nevertheless, when a family first unravels, children feel very wounded and vulnerable— and unloved.

Now is the time for you to lend support, to catch them in your safety net. Give your grandchildren an extra dose of love and "nurturance." If you live nearby, call and visit often. If you live out of town, place frequent phone calls; send letters, cards, packages, and tapes; and make as many long-distance visits as you can muster. Your visits are of special importance during the first year of the separation and divorce, especially those early months. (In chapter 3 there are lists of things to do with or for the grandchildren in the same city or as a long-distance grandparent. The chapter also includes tips for talking with grandchildren about their parents' divorce.)

The grandparents I interviewed and the mental health experts with whom I spoke are all in agreement that with permission (and/ or a request) from one's son or daughter (the custodial parent) as a prerequisite, an active presence at the home of these grandchildren can be of vital importance.

In worst-case scenarios, where there is a wrenching separation or a sudden violent or otherwise traumatic eruption between the two parents, your presence and your ability to take over with the grandchildren becomes of immeasurable value to their inner world.

Bear in mind that a custodial parent in the first throes of the separation may become so inner focused that his or her parenting skills leave something to be desired. While going through the "first degree" or "firsthand" pain, this parent usually does a lot of crying and has an understandable compulsion to talk about what just happened. He or she often feels victimized and may wallow in self-pity. Under these circumstances, it's impossible to listen or hear or react to what is going on with the children.

Until the custodial parent "gets it together," the grandparent can be on hand to determine how the grandchildren are coping with the divorce. Grandchildren *will* signal their feelings both verbally and physically, but it takes a discerning eye and ear to catch this.

Although the grandparent may be in pain as well (chapter 4 deals with this subject in more detail), an objective and compassionate grandparent can probably handle the situation better than the parent in the early stages of the separation. Bonnie Winters, a divorce program specialist at the Aring Institute, discusses the contribution that the grandparent can make:

> *If you can be there to help with the children, the cooking, the driving, the chores, it would be a lifetime gift to your grandchildren. (And your child as well!) It puts into motion the healing process for all*

concerned. You, the grandparent, instead of staying home, wringing your hands, and feeling sorry about it all, can have "hands-on" meaningful tasks to perform, and you will be offering up some emotional security for everyone. . . . Your child's ability as a parent may be somewhat abated; the pain is so great. You as a grandparent can be the barometer, listening to what your grandchildren say and do, and often what they don't say or do.

From my own experience, I can remember that there were times when my grandchildren did not seem to appreciate or understand me or why Mommy wasn't doing things for them. Probably one day they will know and understand. But I kept telling myself that I wasn't there to win applause or plaudits. Don't get waylaid or sidetracked with minutiae. And don't second-guess every decision of the parent in charge. At times, it is better simply to be an interested observer.

The object is not to be deterred from your "mission" or to overreact to their reactions. At times, your grandchildren (and even your own child) may show some resentment toward you as the helping grandparent. And you won't do things "like Mommy does." But take heart. As hostilities and insecurities begin to calm down, everyone's reactive stance will also improve. As one grandmother reflected, "A thick skin is a gift from God!"

As an instrument of recovery for a divided family, you must take on the challenge of trying to restore some balance in the lives of your loved ones and placing them in a stronger position to cope with the changes and adversity they are presently living with.

One grandmother shared her family's story:

When I found out that my son-in-law had left my daughter's home, I flew there as soon as I could. My grandson, a robust and boyish young man of five, had started playing with a boy doll that he had put away when he was three. He was giving baby James a bath, and feeding him and dressing and undressing him, over and over. And when we would go to the mall or the grocery store or out to lunch, he insisted on taking baby James. My daughter was alarmed. But I saw it as acting out the loss of his father and the things he remembered so vividly doing on a daily basis with his dad. My eyes filled up then, as they're doing now. But without making a fuss about baby James, this phase soon passed. It was his way of mourning what once was part of his daily life.

Our little granddaughter, who was then only two and a half, would cry in the night. I can still hear that wail, like that of a small, frail animal, lost in the woods, severed from its paternal influence. With our granddaughter, my husband and I found that simply holding her and reading softly was very helpful.

Everybody in that household, including our daughter, required heavy doses of TLC and one-on-one. We set aside our own active lives for about a month and alternately spent weeks with them. Our daughter, now two years later, revealed to us recently that she feels because of our intervention, involvement, and caring, she and the children were able to accept and recover in a less protracted or hostile way.

Many therapists suggest that, as in any crisis or period of grief, it is best not to pull up roots immediately. They say one should try and keep things as normal as possible for the children by staying in the same house, using the same schools, and keeping things as they were for at least six months to a year, if possible. The only exceptions to this advice would be in cases where there is abusive behavior by the noncustodial parent or where finances dictate a change in living arrangements. Contending with the separation and divorce is more than enough change for the children, advise professionals.

Marc Rabinowitz observes, however, that without any type of support system, either family or good friends, it would be very difficult for the custodial parent and the children to stay in that same community. "If, on the other hand, there are caring family and friends at the home city of the custodial parent, this is an advantage for the entire new family and something to be considered."

The overall consensus is that if you live in another city, you should not overplay your hand, as a parent or grandparent, in pushing for them to come home. Talk to your child about the "options" that he or she has. It must be your child's decision; not yours.

When the crisis erupts, grandparents typically want to visit their distraught son or daughter and grandchildren as soon as possible. In families where the grandparents live out of town, it may take a few days for them to prepare for the trip. In the meantime, there is always the telephone. One grandmother told of speaking to her daughter six or seven times a day, reinforcing the faith in her child's abilities to get through this crisis and to "move on."

When I asked this grandparent what kinds of things she said on the phone, she responded by recalling one prevalent tactic: "Honey, this is a tough time in your life, but we know you are made of strong stuff and you have the courage and wisdom to make it." Several grandparents mentioned that they acted as sounding boards and did very little talking. Just listening is useful. Others spoke of how their children responded. (For example: "Mom, every time I talk with you, I feel stronger and I know I can make it." And "I feel better now, Dad, you have it so logically figured out. I'm OK after hearing how my life *can* work. Yesterday, I was a basket case. Everyday I say to myself, 'I won't let these children down.' ")

One grandfather, Alex, recalled the visit that he and his wife made to see their son and grandchildren:

When we arrived . . . [they] didn't want to see people, even their closest friends. We noticed how our grandchildren were "clingy" and stayed inside the first week or so. But little by little, they ventured into the backyard. Then after a while, they would ride their bikes down the street, but not too far from their house. In a few more days, they were going about their normal routine.

It was interesting to me to see that their state of mourning was much like what we had experienced . . . that pulling in, staying close, "circling the wagons." Their actions and words paralleled our own grieving. We didn't push them; just kept them close, 'til they were ready to test their wings again. Their fear of flying was understandable.

Grandmother Alice:

When I arrived to help get everyone on their feet, my daughter would wake up in the middle of the night and come in my bed. She wanted me to hold her in my arms. Here was this thirty-five-year-old woman, curled up in the fetal position, sobbing her heart out that her life was over! Now that I look back on those days, I wonder where I found the strength to be her strength! I tended to the emotional and physical needs of the children and ran the house, cooked the meals, shopped, and cleaned. When I finally ran out of steam, I arranged for some teenage baby-sitters to come and help out after school, and then I sent for the children's favorite aunt, my sister. Between all of us, working as a team, we were able to put this family back on its feet in weeks. We arranged for family counseling. We found a support group for our daughter and the grandchildren in a single-parent networking group. My husband is still working full-time, so I had to find a neighbor to help our grandson practice for Little League. All this took planning and doing, not just sitting around feeling sorry for ourselves.

Although this grandmother could give her daughter both emotional and physical support, some grandparents cannot comprehend the depth of suffering that their child and grandchildren are experiencing at the onset of the change from a two-parent home to that of a single-parent household. In such cases, counseling with a family therapist or a member of the clergy is advisable.

ROUNDING UP THE FAMILY

As one psychologist noted, "The more people your grandchildren can love and be loved by in return, the better they survive and handle the divorce."

This is the time for extended family. If ever they were needed, it is now—providing, of course, they do not speak disparagingly of the disengaged or custodial parent, or the one who supposedly "broke up the family."

There are many facets of the grandparent-grandchild bond, and one of its most defining features, according to Dr. Ken Lewis, director of Child Custody Services of Philadelphia, Pennsylvania, has to do with a child's roots. In fact, the entire extended family (from great-grandparents and great-aunts and -uncles down to aunts, uncles, and cousins) can serve to reinforce a sense of roots and connectedness. Dr. Lewis asserts that each child has an *implicit* right as written in the First Amendment of our Constitution to the freedom of association with grandparents or other interested and qualified extended family members. "To breach the role of the grandparents in a family, upon divorce," notes Dr. Lewis, "is to make a separate class of children of divorce as opposed to those from intact families." Without such an association, says Dr. Lewis, a child has no awareness of "his heritage, connectedness, cultural roots, familial connection (generation to generation), and what I like to call 'nesting values.' "

As another grandparent adds, "History for your grandchild begins before he or she can remember it." Suggests one grandmother, "A strong extended family, a reaching out to the roots of your beginning, and the knowledge that you are a part of something rather strange, wonderful, and powerful, gives grandchildren a feeling of protectedness. Knowing you fit in a family somewhere gives you a sense of belonging."

The End and the Beginning

Grandparents need to be reminded of the importance of remaining tuned in to the stresses on the single parent, which can be overwhelming. The devastation wrought by the divorce encompasses the custodial parent from the moment of awakening until heavy-lidded eyes close for the night. The partnership of parenting that once existed is no longer. One parent must now handle all the daily chores of the household and child rearing: food preparation, housework, driving to extracurricular activities, discipline, and homework. Younger children need help with baths, dressing and undressing, bedtime rituals, getting ready for school, and so on.

In many cases, these household chores must be juggled with jobs outside the home. Although many parents held paying jobs before the divorce, many others are now going to work for the first time or returning to careers they set aside when their children were born. Outside employment is important not only because the family needs the money but also because it enhances self-esteem (which has taken a beating owing to the separation and divorce). Successes in the workplace and networking with co-workers can help begin the healing.

The single parent may be profoundly lonely, too. Many of his or her close friends may become distant during and after the divorce. There may be a need to network as a single person and to reestablish a tie with the single-adult community. If, as a grandparent, you live in the same city as your son or daughter, watching the grandchildren from time to time, on an occasional evening, offers the custodial parent a much needed respite from child care and enables your child to attend a social function and begin anew as a single.

One single mother confided to me about how she felt in the early stages after her husband moved out. "When my husband left the house and I was alone with the kids each night (with the exception of every other weekend), I dreaded the dinner hour. That empty chair, where he sat across from me, where the kids could reach out and touch him, loomed larger each night until I wanted to throw the damn thing against the window! It got so bad we took to eating on TV trays and watching the tube. At least his absence didn't seem so vivid!"

There are many things that grandparents can do for these single parents. To begin with, adopt a positive attitude. Most therapists believe that you'll accomplish more if you act optimistic about the present and the future. Talking about what might have been is divisive and not in anyone's best interest. Try to keep things on an even keel as much as possible, bringing about some everyday normality that the grandchildren and their parents enjoyed and that the divorce destroyed. Obviously, you will not achieve this goal completely each day, but it is a worthy one to pursue.

If there is more than one child in the household, allow the parent some one-on-one time with each kid. This relieves some of the stress of sibling rivalry and outright fighting, and allows the parent to focus his or her attention on that one child. (It is also very nice for a grandparent and grandchild to be alone together. They can get to know each other better and strengthen the bond between them.)

The old and the young are attracted to one another, according to the experts. A grandchild visiting a grandparent can just "be." There is no need to produce anything. Grandparents, for the most part, are less stressed out than the parent(s). Single parents, especially, who have to make the bulk of the income from which the children live, are often saddled with long hours of work before attending to "their other job" or their "homework."

Grandparents often have more time to do things with children and teach them as well. Some activities that can be shared: baking, repairing broken toys and household items, doing projects and crafts, building model cars, making a dollhouse, gardening, flying a kite, playing checkers and cards, preparing a family dinner. There also appears to be a more relaxed atmosphere at the grandparent's home; less rushing to and from activities and more "tuning in" and listening to the child's conversation and questions. Feeling the absence of the noncustodial parent, the child of divorce can immensely profit from this slower pace and individual attention.

When such a crisis takes place, we have a rare opportunity as grandparents to rebuild our grandchild's self-esteem. For this grandchild has lost a part of himself or herself through the "loss" of a parent from the family unit. Grandparents make the best cheerleaders; they have an unshakable belief in their grandchildren. They can also assure their grandchildren that they are loved and that they did not cause the divorce.

"I love to watch my father watch my children," a parent told me in an interview. "He is fascinated by everything they say and do. And it is evident to me, but more important to them, that he delights in their presence! It's not a bad way to grow up, actually, for what it does for their egos."

In *Family Evaluation in Child Custody: Mediation, Arbitration, and Litigation*, Dr. Richard A. Gardner, a noted child psychiatrist, confirms that a child's involvement with grandparents helps to boost self-esteem:

> *A healthy parent recognizes the importance of the children's having a good relationship with their grandparents. Child therapists do not give the relationship between grandparents and grandchildren the attention they deserve. The enhanced positive regard that grandparents have for their grandchildren contributes to building the children's self-esteem. Grandparents serve as an important buffer to children of divorce. A strongly parental parent will recognize this and do everything to foster good relationships with the grandparents, even after the divorce. (pp. 193–94)*

A word of warning to grandmothers: although involvement with your grandchildren is good, child care may be hazardous to your physical and psychic health. Because women have a long legacy of caring for others at the expense of themselves, you may find yourself overextended in the child-care mode without even realizing it. Well-meaning, busy parents (with grandparents' blessings or acquiescing at times) begin to slip into a dependency pattern, and before you know it, you're raising children all over again!

As grandparents relate to the new single-parent family, they will not always see eye-to-eye with their son or daughter on child rearing. There is usually a generational difference: the old way versus the new way. The parent says, "This is how I want to raise my children." The grandparent counters, "But they're my grandchildren, and this is how I think they should be raised." But just because grandparents see things differently from parents, this does not mean that one party is right and the other is wrong. According to Harriet Goldhor Lerner, in her popular book *Dance of Anger*, "It's that all people think, feel and react differently" (p. 39).

Whether or not you agree with your son or daughter's methods of child rearing is not as pivotal as how the differences are handled. You must work things out for the sake of those grandchildren. (But don't subject grandchildren to a show of ill feeling between you and their parent.) Perhaps some professional counseling may be needed in order to improve or resolve the situation. It is easy to infringe on the parent's territory, without meaning to do so.

Grandparents may also have differences with their offspring over the latter's lifestyle. It's best if grandparents can keep negative comments to a minimum, but in cases where grandparents are extremely uncomfortable with this lifestyle, they may need to speak up and be frank—especially when they feel there will be a harmful effect on the grandchildren. This advice was given to me by family therapist Marc Rabinowitz, who suggests thinking along these lines: "Say to yourself, 'I wouldn't support this behavior if he or she was single, so I certainly wouldn't do so when there are children involved.' "

According to most psychologists, the hostility exhibited by

adult children when their parents give them advice is due in part to their bruised ego. The ego is affected not only by the divorce itself but also by a renewed dependency on the older generation (after finally achieving autonomy). This is a step backward in the child-parent relationship. As the late child psychiatrist Dr. Haim Ginott wrote in his book *Between Parent and Child*, "dependency breeds hostility."

As the new single-parent family evolves, the role of a grandparent will also evolve. Professionals warn us not to undermine the autonomy of the custodial parent and his or her role as the primary caretaker and person in control of the children. The parent must set the parameters of child care. You are there in an auxiliary role and as a support personage. You are not there to take over. In the initial stages of the separation and divorce, your son or daughter may call upon you as a surrogate parent or to do some coparenting, but as time heals the wound, your intense involvement should ebb and a more natural state of grandparenting can take place.

The micromanagement of a son or daughter's home and every household or child-care decision is detrimental to the adult child's healing and growth, as well as setting up a confusing host of "parents" for your grandchildren.

One grandmother told this story:

I was driving my grandson home after caring for him for part of an afternoon, and he began to take some candy from his school bag. It was close to dinner, and I said something like, "I can't believe she lets him have candy before dinner!" I was already ticked off about other things that had occurred that week, all of which I viewed as permissive child care. I said something to the effect that "your mother sure does some strange things," and my grandson piped up, "But Nanny, she's the best mother for me!" Out of the mouths of babes! From then on I never said a thing that was the slightest [bit] demeaning or critical about his mother . . . my daughter. We talk things out, my daughter and I, without the kids around, and when we have differences about discipline, food, or anything concerning them, we work it out.

From the counselors, family therapists, social workers, and support groups, the word is out: "Grandchildren need to see grandparents and parents as allies, not enemies!" Children have an amazing facility, they say, to perceive, even from innuendo and nuance, how one adult feels about another. As a young grandchild said plaintively to her grandmother, "Don't you like my mommy?"

Sally Brush, of the Aring Institute, gives the following advice: "Status reports when mother comes to pick them up, unless favorable, are best conveyed when you and the grandchild's mother (or father) are speaking in private. And even then, do not embellish the grandchildren's wrongdoings when they are in your care. If you have to, try this approach: 'This is an observation I have made about Jane.' This is a more neutral and less threatening stance than a pronouncement about the child's behavior."

Brush also recommends that you tell your son or daughter in the early stages of this renewed relationship: "As a parent of a grown child, I have the right to make suggestions to you [about child care], and you have the duty to listen to them. You have the right to accept or reject my suggestions, *respectfully*, and then I must abide by your decision."

A method that works for one grandmother, who "minds" her granddaughter from three to five o'clock each weekday, goes something like this. " 'My mommy doesn't make me wash my hands before I eat,' my granddaughter said on the first day of coming here. I explained that my ways and her mother's were different, and that just like school, each teacher has her own rules and you soon learn how to respect and get along with each teacher by knowing what each one expects!"

Gerontologist Timothy Brubaker of Miami University believes that parents of adult children should not offer to do anything that they really don't want to do or that they can't afford to do. (The younger generation should think about how their requests affect their parents, as well.) "Whenever possible," he suggests, "what needs to be done, or who will do what and how much, etc., needs to be negotiated early on."

There is almost complete agreement among therapists that getting along with the custodial parent translates into achieving a more functional and stable environment for the grandchildren. Grandparents, in tandem with the grandchildren's parents, must unite for the common goal of giving each grandchild that safe haven—and a new beginning. And besides, it's in everyone's best interest to do so.

2.
The
"Rescue" Operation

❦

Whether you throw them a life preserver, race out in a rowboat, or just extend your arm, the waters can be as treacherous for the rescuer as for the rescuee. Tread lightly, say the professionals, as you approach the newly divided family.

Bonnie Winters, a divorce program specialist at the Aring Institute, dislikes the connotation of the word "rescue." "I think rescuing per se is demeaning. Divorce is a disempowering experience anyway, with low self-esteem following on its heels."

"What would you do for your best friend?" asks Winters. "You would more than likely say, 'Where do you need me?' I doubt whether you would rush in and take over or give unsolicited advice. Your son or daughter can be made to feel helpless by being 'rescued.' With rescue, there are often strings attached, which sets up problems between the adult child and the parent. You don't have to step in to bail them out to show your unconditional love."

Speaking of unconditional love, Jane Kaminski, who works for a family services agency in Virginia, declares that such love "is far more important than whether or not you can give your grandchildren the latest in tennis shoes! Every grandparent can give something of himself or herself." The sentiments expressed by Winters and Kaminski are shared by a wide number of psychologists and psychiatrists.

"Massive caretaking is just about as bad as doing nothing," observes Dr. Charles Parker, a Virginia psychiatrist. "But teaching your child and grandchildren about how life works—that life is inherently fraught with change—that we have to expect it and adapt to it—is what we can do in our role as grandparental teachers, rather than rescuers," says Dr. Parker. He also asserts that we grandparents should be available to the degree that we are comfortable with. "Negotiate it out and set boundaries, or you will develop an overreliance [in your child]."

It may be appropriate at this juncture to refer to Dr. Parker's remark in chapter 1 about trying to remove *all* the pain of your divorcing child. He feels that even if you could remove all the pain, the "taking over" of this pain would be resented by your child for a lifetime. "He or she has to handle it!" insists Dr. Parker.

The consensus of many therapists is that where there is extensive rescuing of an adult child going through a divorce, the result tends to be not only an overreliance on parent(s) but also a lack of acceptance of the situation. This only perpetuates a continuation of denial that "this happened to *me*, and *I* have to deal with it." Such denial, say the experts, can last a lifetime and impair maturity.

Family members are usually unprepared for the extent of the pain and the length of time it takes to recover in a divorce, declare the mental health specialists. If we, as parents, can better understand the emotional process of our child's divorce, we will be less unsettled by what we see and hear and can thus more realistically provide emotional support and other practical assistance to strengthen this family.

As noted earlier, a divorce is comparable to death. The grief process is much the same. First comes denial, then anger, bargaining, depression, and finally acceptance. These steps may not necessarily come in this order. And for some they may come a few at a time or all at once. Your adult child may get over one or two and still have to deal with the others for a while longer. The experts plead for our patience and understanding. Recovery works, they say, but it can take years.

In the pursuit of a measure of constancy—of normalcy—for the sake of our grandchildren, we must take heed of the wisdom of Dr. Arthur Kornhaber, founder of the grandparent movement. In his book *Grandparents/Grandchildren: The Vital Connection*, and in his years of practice as a child psychiatrist, he speaks about the necessity of shoring up this divided family—of buttressing this weakened foundation—not just by coming to the aid of the grandchildren but by supporting and respecting the son or daughter, who must travail against the odds. He implores us to empathize with, and understand the challenge of, the adult child's new role as a single parent, usually a *working* single parent. This role entails dealing with all the pitfalls and awesome responsibilities of raising children alone while maintaining both home and career. Showing love, attentiveness, and concern to this adult child may help him or her to summon up courage and abilities to get the job done. Any form of rescue, help, or assistance for grandchildren must coexist with support of the parent.

EMOTIONAL SUPPORT

What Grandparents Can Do

Although you need to quell the storm and reawaken your nurturing skills, there is a consensus among the professionals that what you *really* need to convey to your adult child is your willingness to understand and be there if and when you're needed, at least in the beginning days.

Especially in the early stages of the divorce, the needs of your adult child are immense. Your child may be severely depressed—so much so that he or she is not really functioning. You will probably have to be there (if you possibly can) to assist with the grandchildren.

Jennette Franklin, a social worker who practices in Virginia, aptly describes the situation:

> Because of the emotional circumstances at home, your adult child and grandchildren are living in a dysfunctional and chaotic world. There's a lot of weeping, very little normalcy of routine; meals are a catch-as-catch-can situation—an if or when, or more like a maybe occurrence. If rescuing means Grandma (and Grandpa?) can take the children for a short visit, then I'm all for it, providing, of course, the children have a close and warm relationship with the grandparent(s). The custodial parent, usually your adult child, could have some time to himself or herself, to perhaps seek out counseling and a support group, interview attorneys [see discussion in the following sections], and analyze their situation. Just to be able to focus on their hurt and mourn without having to worry about the children would be a godsend.

The extent of your involvement is very much predicated on having a decent relationship with your child. While your intervention as your child's and grandchild's advocate may be necessary, albeit temporary, much of what you will accomplish rests on your having the trust of your son or daughter.

Marc Rabinowitz, a family therapist, differentiates methods of help:

> You need to continue to reinforce what your adult child wants, rather than take this as an opportunity just to jump in. Such as:

"We're available and you need to decide what you would like us to do. This is your family. We can be a support for you, but we aren't going to take over for you."

Listen, it's normal for you to want to take care of your adult child. He or she is hurting. But you want to work through your adult child, rather than go around them. This reinforces his or her parenting abilities to make decisions which will ultimately help that adult child get over this crisis more quickly rather than if someone takes over completely.

So—what, precisely, can you do to help? Divorce group leaders at the Aring Institute recommend that you encourage your child in behavior that has proven helpful in these circumstances: exercising, gardening, telling the story of the divorce to a trusted friend, writing in a journal, working on artistic endeavors, connecting with a loved one, and, yes, crying!

Many grandparents, drawing from their own experience, say that one of your greatest contributions is getting your son or daughter (and grandchildren) to eat well. Sometimes, when your child is out of sync in those early days, weeks, or months, planning a meal—no less cooking it—adds to his or her depression, for your child remembers only too well that person who once shared the meals and maybe the cooking as well.

Your adult child will probably exhibit contradictory feelings and thoughts during the separation and divorce and for a while afterward. There may even be physical symptoms in tandem with the emotional upset or occurring periodically during the grief process. These symptoms may include insomnia, nausea, diarrhea, severe constipation and stomach cramping, fatigue, difficulty in concentration, and a change in appetite—bouts of overeating or days of scarcely ingesting any food at all. Most of the time these physical manifestations are part of the reaction to the chaotic and drastic life changes that are unfolding.

The "Rescue" Operation

Counseling and/or a Support Group

Most therapists agree on the importance of counseling for an individual going through a divorce. So you can perform a valuable service by painstakingly, quietly, and carefully pointing your adult child in this direction.

The experts are less sanguine about seeking counseling for the grandchildren. Franklin feels that for the young ones to alleviate some of their stress, they need to be able to express their hurt, their anger, and their confusion. "It does not have to be professional counseling. If there is a caring minister, grandparent, friend, aunt, or teacher—someone that the children are close to and communicate well with—then this will usually suffice. Children need to examine their confusion and their pain. And most often, they don't have the coping skills to deal with anger in constructive ways. Children have not yet acquired the skills of processing things out."

Marc Rabinowitz concurs:

With the grandchildren, I'm not so quick to jump into therapy because there are already a lot of changes going on in their lives and I'm reluctant to introduce new people into the children's lives. That is, of course, if the parents can parent. Having the custodial parent and the children together in therapy helps the transition from a two-parent home into a single one. Of course, the ideal would be to bring the noncustodial parent into counseling as well. However, this is usually hard to do, especially in the beginning when there is so much anger. But it's a goal worth striving for down the road.

Nonetheless, it's complicated. It really depends a lot on the degree of trauma at the time of the divorce. Grandparents may have to do some decision making as to what it is in the best interest of the grandchildren if the parent(s) are overly consumed, in extensive treatment, or unable to cope. All of this is in accordance with the severity of the facts. In the early stages of the separation, let things settle down at first before bringing the children into therapy. The parent probably needs it right away. I like to reinforce existing structures and emphasize improving parenting in the early months.

Your adult child may be so damaged and distraught that he or she may not be able to make wise decisions in these early stages. According to Franklin, "Anyone divorcing needs to know how to get the best professional help. It is a disaster to select a therapist (or a lawyer) from the Yellow Pages! Credentials are important, but they need to find someone they can be comfortable with as they will be spending a lot of time with these people. And being able to relate is half the battle. You the parent-grandparent, may have to do some of the initial research and perhaps be their resource person, especially if your adult child (the custodial parent) is dysfunctional, as is often the case."

Many professionals recommend that if you're looking for a family therapist, try to find one who is a clinical member of the American Association for Marriage and Family Therapy.

Bonnie Winters of the Aring Institute notes that there are many psychiatric nurses and social workers with experience and expertise in handling divorce counseling. The main thing is to meet with this person and to feel comfortable with him or her before embarking on a series of therapy sessions.

Jane Kaminski explains that there is a time when counseling is appropriate and that seeking counseling is an individual decision. Rather than seeing an individual counselor, some individuals may prefer to join a support group. And some people decide to combine counseling with a support group.

Attending support groups can be particularly helpful, for sharing experiences with others who have been in the same boat diminishes the pain. "When you are in a support group," says Kaminski, "you find yourself normalized. It's real important for your adult child, going through the divorce, to get together with people who are in similar situations. Where there is no support network in your community, you need to develop an informal network. Contact

United Way, your religious affiliation, community centers, et cetera. Newspapers today list public service announcements and usually have a list of meetings and support groups in your area."

Kaminski suggests that grandparents do no more than suggest to the adult child that he or she may need therapy or a support group. Otherwise, she claims, it's overstepping one's bounds. "But when they are ready for networking and/or therapy, you can try and locate some of the resources such as 'Parents Without Partners' or other single-parent support groups. What you are trying to do is to steer them in a direction that will be helping themselves."

Kaminski drives home the point: "*Give* a man a fish, you feed him for a day. Teach him *how* to fish, you feed him for life. In order to restore the independence of your adult child," Kaminski pointedly adds, "it is not the grandparents' province to do otherwise."

Divorce is a "life stressor." Everyone will probably be out of balance for a while. But as Jennette Franklin tells her clients— people going through divorce—as well as their parents, who often accompany them into her office: "People, this may be a crazy time, but it doesn't mean *you're* crazy!"

LEGAL AND/OR MEDIATION SERVICES

How to find a lawyer who will handle the divorce? Here is some advice you may wish to pass on to your adult child, *if* he or she needs and wants it. The following tips are offered by a longtime family law practitioner, William B. Smith of Virginia.

§ Look for a divorce or matrimonial lawyer or someone steeped in family law. (In some areas of the country, this field of law is known as domestic relations.)

§ Get a recommendation from a friend or acquaintance who

has been in a similar situation. A satisfied client is the best source for finding a lawyer.

✎ Check your local bar association and state bar referral services. For the first consultation, a modest fee is usually charged. This fee is not for the lawyers but simply to maintain the service. In most cases, the referral service gives you the names of three attorneys experienced in a given field of law.

✎ Look through *Martindale-Hubbell Lawyers' Directory*, a reference book available in most public libraries and in local law libraries. (In many areas of the country, law libraries are open to the public.) This book contains ratings of local lawyers and lists their specialties and professional credentials.

✎ Read the ads for attorneys in the yellow pages of your phone directory. But bear in mind that just because a lawyer runs an ad, he or she is not necessarily qualified or certified in the field of family law. The best way to find out is to ask for client references.

✎ Check with your son or daughter's family therapist or a family service agency for a recommendation of one or more lawyers in a family law practice.

✎ Call upon a clerk in the office of the family court or domestic relations court. Or an intake person or one of the judges may point the way for your son or daughter to locate an attorney who is experienced in family law. Ask for the names of three competent lawyers experienced in family law.

✎ The American Trial Lawyers Association or a state trial lawyers association may have a list of lawyers who specialize in family law and who are also experienced in the courtroom with custody, visitation, and support disputes.

✎ If you have a family lawyer or a lawyer-friend and your adult child lives in another city or state, ask this attorney if he or she has any personal contacts or can recommend the services of an attorney in the area where your son or daughter resides.

❧ When considering an attorney, ask the following questions: what are the hourly and the daily fees? Is there a charge for phone advice as well? What is the difference in fees for in-court versus out-of-court representation? What is the cost of a hearing before a divorce commissioner? How much would an appeal cost? What type of payment plan is available? And above all, what is the lawyer's experience in family law matters?

Smith believes that the main criteria in selecting a lawyer are to feel comfortable with the attorney and to find someone who has experience in family law and charges reasonable fees. Because the issues of custody, visitation, and support are so important and complicated (plus laden with emotion), it is in the best interests of the custodial parent and your grandchildren, says Smith, to have *adequate* legal representation.

When a wife and husband who very well may be the mother and father of your grandchildren have bickered for years, and now agree to divorce, it may be the only thing they have agreed on in a while. With some cautious nudging by the lawyers, they will split their property, dissolve the marriage, and go their separate ways. However, parenthood will keep them in contact. How will they decide issues like child support, spousal support, custody, and visitation?

Therapists believe that children whose parents continue their hostilities after divorcing have a greater chance of suffering adjustment problems than those whose parents are able to agree on post-divorce arrangements. Research has shown that a civil parent-to-parent relationship following a divorce is important to a child's well-being. A process known as mediation can set the stage for such a relationship far better than the adversarial system.

Advocates of mediation claim it saves time, for most states have overcrowded court dockets. And the process can save the parties several hundred dollars by avoiding litigation. But the reason most often given by proponents of mediation is that it is of direct benefit to children since it keeps the parties amicable for long periods of time.

If Mom and Dad can keep talking, airing their differences around a conference table instead of in a courtroom, children of this marriage may suffer less. Mediators at the Aring Institute find that with family mediation, children adjust better and fathers improve their performance in paying child support. Furthermore, parental cooperation is reinforced, and visitation is encouraged.

Family law specialist and divorce mediator Tazewell T. Hubard III of Virginia had this to say on the issue: "I believe mediation decreases the chance of exacerbation of hostilities and heightens awareness of what is in the best interest of the children, as opposed to the adversarial process. Mediation gets the couple beyond thinking of themselves and brings the focus to the children and what is best for them. In my experience, mediation transforms the parties from husband and wife to being *parents*. Mediation says: 'What can we do? What can I do? As parents—or as a parent—for the welfare of our child—my child?' "

Many members of the legal community with whom I talked who favor either private or court-mandated mediation in family matters concede that the traditional adversary process is an effective method of dispute resolution when *no* continuing relationship between the warring parties is necessary. But divorcing parents need to cooperate in the future for the benefit of their children. Mediation of support, custody, and visitation issues can preserve and enhance this part of their relationship, they claim.

Mediation supporters say it is far better for both parties to reach a conclusion by negotiation and consent rather than having the decision imposed on the parties by a court. With mediation, each party accepts and can live with the outcome; with litigation, there is a winner and a loser.

In addition, mediation gives divorcing couples a sense of self-determination and accomplishment. The relationship is not so much "severed," claims one attorney; it is simply "transformed."

Some of the parents I interviewed who utilized either private or court mediation found it to be a positive force in keeping their family alive and well and felt it resolved many conflicts in a sensitive and private way that inspired compromise.

A number of family law attorneys have become private mediators in recent years. Some work alone; others work in tandem with a family therapist. After an agreement is reached, the mediator must write it up in legal form to be reviewed by the couple's attorneys. (Each spouse must have a separate attorney review the agreement.) The mediation agreement is then incorporated into the divorce decree after a judicial review.

Therapist Don Mohr of California uses the attorney-therapist approach with his wife, Elizabeth Allen, who is an attorney-mediator. "In divorce mediation," Mohr says, "the point is to help people undo emotional roadblocks." Mohr works to keep the focus off "who is the bad guy" and tries to frame issues positively in order to keep the focus on the team that will go forward as parents. Many lawyers and social workers who function as mediators favor the attorney-therapist approach.

Generally, mediation is successful in about 70 to 80 percent of cases. But even when the parties do not reach an agreement, "they learn to communicate better and to put the issues on the table," note Mohr and Allen.

There appears to be a varying degree of mediation from state to state. Some mediation programs are mandated by legislation, some by court rule, some just by policy. "Mandatory" in these programs means participants must meet with a court mediator (usually two or three times) to try to resolve the dispute. If a solution cannot be reached, the parties proceed to litigation.

Michael McCurley, a Dallas attorney, chairman of the Family Law Section of the Texas State Bar and a member of the mediation committee of the American Academy of Matrimonial Lawyers, worries that mediation does not always provide a level playing field. "There is a bias against women in the process of mediation," says McCurley. Other attorneys agree that sometimes the parties in a dispute cannot be made into participants with equal bargaining power. These attorneys speak to the general assumption that men have superior knowledge about the estate, better access to lawyers, and are likely to be more aggressive in the relationship.

Tazewell Hubard, on the other hand, believes that mediation empowers both parties on a fairly equal basis.

I find mediation good for the female. She may have very little experience in handling assets, i.e., stock portfolio, etcetera. She may not even be knowledgeable in balancing the checkbook or know of the assets of the marriage. But when I have this wife and her husband around the mediating table, we openly identify property rights, financial rights, evaluate the division of property. There is legal closure and emotional closure. Furthermore, I believe for mediation to succeed, the wife must be as empowered as her husband and understand their collective worth. A competent mediator knows how to deal with family dynamics, a vital part of which is money. The mediator should make certain the power is in balance, especially if one of the parties is not on an equal plane.

But some women's rights groups have recently suggested changing or abandoning mediation in family law cases. They cite at least fourteen reports, eight by task forces studying state courts, that show women have less bargaining power than do men in the mediation process.

In cases where domestic violence exists, mediation can make the situation worse, believes Dianne Post, an attorney in Phoenix, Arizona. She asserts that court-ordered mediation in these types of

cases often produces more violence during the mediation sessions
or directly afterward. Some opponents of mediation in domestic
violence cases claim that maintaining the relationship in the case
of battered women means increasing the risk of more injury. A
Harvard study found more domestic abuse after mediation sessions
than after trial.

Hubard explains that a good lawyer-mediator can go to court
and ask for a protective order, which is a legal means of keeping a
husband, with a history of violence, away from the wife.

*If this order is violated, the husband can be incarcerated and also be
held in contempt of court.*

*There are checks and balances. I work with a therapist in cases
where there is abusive behavior. The therapist keeps me informed if
there are any threats or increased negative behavior or heavy bouts
of drinking. As a prerequisite to mediation in these types of cases, I
have the parties go into therapy separately and jointly.*

*When one of the parties refuses to seek therapy or halt their
objectionable behavior, I cease the mediation and refer this case on
to social services and let the traditional court process take over.*

*My advice to your adult child seeking mediation is to look for
someone who has had therapeutic training in combination with the
legal skills of mediation.*

Attorney Mary G. Commander, who handles a wide variety of
family law matters, has another point of view: "The only mediation
that I see that works is where both parties are fairly reasonable
people. They go into mediation because they can't communicate.
But a batterer, in rehab or not, is a batterer! And in mediation, he
shows resentment at his loss of control. Why should the wife have
to sit there and be afraid of her spouse? I don't believe in mediation
in cases where there is a history of violent behavior."

Post insists that mediation must reflect trust, understanding,
and goodwill. "Parties must freely agree to cooperate and compro-

mise. . . . [They] should have equal power, knowledge, and communication skills. Since none of the above is true in cases of domestic violence, mandatory mediation is a contradiction in terms."

More than twelve states now prohibit mediation in domestic violence cases. And in some states, parties may be exempt from mediation if it would cause undue hardship.

"In one sense," says Post, "mediation and alternative dispute resolution shows the feminist influence in law. Women are not so adversarial. But on the other hand, these methods do not work for oppressed groups. Maybe we're just in a cycle we have to get through before women's rights can be assured."

Ohio attorney Denise Mirman, former chair of the American Trial Lawyers Family Law Section, is concerned about assuring the rights of both parties in any mediation forum. "Mediation should not take place until both parties consult with their attorneys to find out what their rights are," she contends.

Mediation is now available in public and private forums in almost every state. At least thirty-five states and the District of Columbia have some form of court-based mediation program for domestic relations cases. (See chapter 6 for information on mediation for grandparents regarding visitation and custody matters.)

FINANCIAL ASSISTANCE

Money Talks: Getting the Divided Family
over the Hump

As life expectancy has lengthened, grandmas and grandpas have more zest for life, but their financial expenses can be considerable. They may still have children at home and/or in college who require financial support. They may be shouldering all the costs of caring for aging parents. And if one of their children divorces, they may be giving financial assistance to this son or daughter and any children from the marriage. No wonder we term this generation of grandparents the "sandwiched" generation. (I liken it to a "triple-decker!")

Jennette Franklin, a social worker, asserts that

You can only cut the pie [in] so many ways. I have to counsel the parents [of divorcing children] in setting limits on financial requests. Many of them get in too deep and can't say no. When parents need to subsidize children, I advise two things. [First,] be careful not to get into the rescue mode. Sit down with your adult child and figure out how much you can afford. I advise families who are helping out financially to come up with a set amount they can handle (on a weekly or monthly basis) and let the adult child going through the divorce manage the money.

However, in some cases where your son or daughter cannot manage money, the point is to make sure you state that you will have to look at this in three months or six months. "We need to sit down and look at this and see how our finances are holding up, dear" is the approach I counsel.

[The second thing I advise is] always to leave the door open. I find that when grandparents are not in a circumstance to help significantly to maintain their son or daughter and grandchildren in the style of living [to which] they once were [accustomed], they often find themselves with tremendous guilt feelings. Let go of the guilt.

Money is one of the most difficult things for parents and grandparents to sit down and discuss. The adult child needs to be made aware of other elements such as the cost of keeping great-grandmother in a caring facility, or the needs of other siblings, and of course, the retirement plans (and savings) of their parents.

"Like everything else in life, keep things open to renegotiation," adds family therapist Marc Rabinowitz. "Going overboard in a crisis—you can't sustain it. Don't feel you are locked into anything."

Here are a few examples of monetary forms of rescue frequently undertaken by grandparents:

Mortgage payments. *My ex-son-in-law paid the lowest amount of child support that he could legally get away with. And no spousal support! Our daughter had two young children back then and had no job for about the first six months after the divorce. She couldn't pay the mortgage, and the house would have been foreclosed. My wife and I didn't want her to lose the only financial security she really had. So we scraped together enough money to pay that mortgage until the house was sold.*

Paying the rent. *We paid our daughter's rent after the divorce for about four months or so, just till she found a decent job. And we [still] help out occasionally with unusual expenses that they run into now and then. But hey, the way I look at it—they're getting their inheritance while we can see them reap the pleasure.*

Food, clothes, and after-school care. *We tried to help our son and our grandchildren. They weren't in very good financial shape. Our ex-daughter-in-law was the main breadwinner, and their support share wasn't all that great. They had to move from their home into an apartment. But we helped out with meals, with some of the clothing needs of the grandchildren, and with after-school care.*

Paying for visits. *When our ex-daughter-in-law declared she wanted a divorce, we made a point of seeing our son and the grandchildren at least once a month. It wasn't cheap to get there. But we did it to give them our emotional support. Financially? Well— whenever we were there for a visit, we'd buy the kids some needed clothes or things for school or something for the place. I'd come loaded down with some home-cooked food: a turkey roast and all the trimmings—cakes and pies and a few frozen dinners for our son to keep on hand. The kids would be so excited! They still talk about how when we came it was Thanksgiving—even if the calendar said*

July! Every holiday we sent them tickets to come and be with us—to be with the family. This, I think, was our greatest financial contribution. That extended family was so important back then—to those kids. We've built up a sense of family in those little ones, and the aunts, uncles, and cousins (our other kids and their children) are reaching out.

Day-care expenses. *I thought I could help out this newly divorced family by keeping our youngest grandchild with me during the day while my daughter works. That's how it started out. But when my husband became ill, I could no longer manage both. So we found, through our local family services (a United Way agency) an excellent day-care program for working parents. You pay on a sliding scale. This is our contribution. It's all we can do—but at least it's something. Now all I have to do is work on getting rid of the guilt for not being able to do more!*

So yes, Virginia, money talks and gets them over the hump in those early days. It's not only a noble gesture but, more than likely, a necessary one. In the beginning months, the support payments may not have "kicked in." Sometimes the court machinery in various states may be ponderous. And where there is a protracted divorce, the flow of dollars can be delayed. Whatever the reason, not excluding the deadbeat parent, you and your financial commitment are probably a lifesaver!

Look at the Entire Financial Picture

As stated in the first paragraph of this chapter, rescuing poses dangers for the rescuer as for the rescuee. As far as financial support is concerned, you may be committing yourself to a long-term weekly or monthly amount of money without realizing you are doing so and without regard to your overall financial picture.

As one accountant candidly asked, "What would happen if your spouse were to be left a widow or widower? Would this financial commitment to your adult child and grandchildren continue while still allowing your spouse to live within the style of living to which he or she is accustomed? And have you provided for long-term care for you and your spouse as a couple, or as widow and widower?"

This accountant advises: "Prioritize your finances and know thyself and thy resources! Try and figure out how close you are to retirement and what benefits, including social security, you will have to live on."

Experts in the financial field recommend that before meeting face-to-face with your adult son or daughter and discussing financial assistance (not to mention deciding on how much and for how long to give), you should meet with an accountant or financial adviser and appraise the estate. Look at the entire spectrum of your finances: from investments and retirement plans to mortgage and even insurance. If you and/or your spouse are employed, consider how many more years you have until retirement, and how much money will be generated in the interim. For a monthly source of income, look into taking out a reverse mortgage. (Be sure to check out this option with your financial planner. For further information about reverse mortgages, here is a toll-free number: 1-800-285-0618.)

At the Aring Institute, Sally Brush is a facilitator for a grand-parents' support group. She says that "there appears to be a lot of guilt by grandparents who have a strong desire to help their adult child with attorney fees and with the settling-in process. But at the same time, they appear to have big worries themselves about having enough dollars for retirement and medical bills."

Here is what Marc Rabinowitz has to say on this subject: "Setting limits as to amount [of money] and length of time [it will be given] may be wise so as not to impinge on future retirement plans. The parents, at this point in time, are usually in the stage of planning their retirement; if not already in that stage. It is a stage of life where planning for one's estate is essential."

Beware of Creating an Overdependency

Without setting financial limits, you'll be harming your adult child as well as yourself. Stanwood Dickman, accountant, says: "[Ask yourself], Am I creating an overdependency for my adult child? Will my aid prevent my child from learning how to live within his or her means and to make the necessary sacrifices it takes to learn to live within the income one produces? It can't be a one-way street! Does my help cancel out in any way his or her initiative?"

When financial assistance has "strings attached," adult children become even more resentful, and their parents are inevitably disappointed. In Sally Brush's grandparents' support group, the participants "expect their advice will be listened to and be more acceptable because of the giving of money. But when we actually talk about how this plays out, most of the grandparents say it seldom works out this way. As one grandparent noted, 'It's strictly fantasizing to think your son or daughter will parent the children and live their life according to your plan just because you're helping out!' "

Haim Ginott's theory that "dependency breeds hostility" is borne out in many interviews with grandparents and practitioners. Rabinowitz suggests that we regard financial support in the same way we look at alimony or spousal support—"It's temporary until they get back on their feet. Job training, moving, et cetera."

"You have to draw a line in the sand," he said, "but who draws the line? To avoid this dilemma, communication seems to be a prerequisite for having meaningful discussions about how much financial assistance the parents are capable of doing, or what to do. I think it is helpful for the parents of the adult child not to be overgenerous in ways that will set up too much dependency and take away the adult child's initiative to work, to make sacrifices, to move on in his or her career, etc."

We grandparents need to determine whether or not this is a transitional arrangement. What are the circumstances that would entail extending financial help or curtailing it? The experts say to discuss all these points openly with your adult child.

How can you, an interested and concerned grandparent, help this parent and grandchild without damaging the ego of this custodial parent or creating more dependency? Grandparents must find ways of making their aid more palatable, say the behaviorists. There are ways, they claim, whereby we can use our money wisely: to create independence rather than dependence. One suggestion is to perhaps improve your son or daughter's career opportunities. Money for job training is an investment in your adult child, and in the long haul should point him or her toward the goal of financial independence.

Holiday gift giving, as well as birthdays, can be more expansive to include gifts of needed clothing such as a winter coat, shoes, or a special outfit (for your adult child, as well as the grandchildren!). Or an offer of two weeks of summer camp for the grandchildren, or a vacation with Grandma and Grandpa. These are just some of the ways of giving money without an accompanying loss of dignity. A gift of *time*—precious hours with your grandchildren—does not carry a huge price tag.

More Bits and Pieces of Advice

In an interview with Stanwood Dickman, a Virginia accountant, I received some valuable financial advice, which I am happy to pass along to you:

Can you talk about the most intimate details of your financial picture with your adult child? . . . If you can't, you need a third party who can, such as your accountant or financial planner. What I'm saying, in essence, is that you will need a financial manager for this adult child, presupposing that he or she cannot do this on their own. This person should be someone who is familiar with the grandparent's financial position, who is a good communicator, and who knows your adult child, at least on a peripheral basis. Sometimes having a third party, such as the family accountant, takes the uneasiness away from the financial discourse and disclosure.

Help your adult child make a budget—how much are they bringing in; what are their expenses? What frills can be cut out? Before you make a commitment to help them, you should review the budget together. You try and get them to learn to live within their means, as much as possible, when reviewing the budget.

It's part of life—being candid [about finances] with your adult children, and the grandchildren if they are old enough. The grandchildren can be brought into some of the discussion. Their demands can sometimes be butted by reality—by being made aware of their true financial picture, without undue alarm, of course, or injecting any further insecurity in the child.

Your adult child, whom you are trying to assist, needs a true "reality check" concerning their own finances, as well as your own on a periodic basis.

The first step is to cut down the living expenses. The living arrangement—rent or mortgage—is your single, largest expense. Maybe your adult child can share the apartment or home with a roommate; maybe another mother who is in the same boat. This would cut the expenses in half. Maintenance, monthly payments for utilities, rent or mortgage payment, even the cost of food could be split.

You cannot always count on support payments. Therefore, budgets should not necessarily reflect this as income. This is especially true if there is a pattern of nonpayment built up over the months. However, there is garnishment of wages in place now in most states for the family to receive support monies owed them. In addition, the IRS is now assisting states in locating delinquent support payments.

[Concerning medical insurance]: Does your son or daughter have adequate medical insurance in his or her job that also covers your grandchildren?

What is your proximity to medical care and cost of supplemental B coverage to medicare? Don't let your coverage slip.

I recommend long-term health care insurance that would assuage the grandparents' health problems if they were to occur and the nursing-home care for the great-grandparent, in the even this becomes necessary. The likelihood of people living into their nineties is on the rise.

Since you are the provider, sit down with that custodial parent. They have to share their financial problems with you in black and white. If you are the provider in this case, you have to see where they're coming from. Then you can interrelate these facts in your own mind with what you can afford, assuming you are in any position to even make a commitment.

Write the Social Security Administration to find out what your retirement income will be. You need to have a picture in your own mind and be aware of the type of social security benefits you can look to down the road. Then we incorporate this into our thinking about how we will balance this help with planning for illness, retirement, loss of work, and our "golden years"—or, as they used to say, our "old age."

Parents of adult children are often in their sixties or seventies. They are fearful of getting sick and not having adequate resources necessary to sustain themselves in their own capacity. This should somehow be conveyed to the adult child you are trying to assist.

Talk to your adult child about your foremost responsibility, which is to your spouse. You do not want to jeopardize in any way this coverage in your desire to maintain the adult child and grandchildren. You need to communicate this to your child; this peace of mind that you want for your mate.

The "Rescue" Operation

You may wish to leave your liquid assets untouched and use an investment that throws off a monthly amount of funds to be ear-marked for the assistance of your adult child and grandchildren.

Your child would have a better feeling about themselves if they can learn to manage money. Give them so much a month or for six months or for a year so they can turn dependency into dignity instead of just doling out money per week or per bill.

Summing up, I would reiterate that [you should] know well your own financial condition before you make the decision to assist. Come back and review your goal. What should it take to make this par-ent—this adult child—as self-sufficient as possible while not imping-ing upon the financial security of you and your spouse and yet offer-ing some financial equilibrium for your child and grandchild?

3.
Life Support Systems

§

BUILDING POSITIVE

RELATIONSHIPS

As we have seen, during and immediately after the divorce parents are often too preoccupied with their own troubles to respond with pleasure to anything, including their children. This deprives children of a major source of self-esteem—the ability to see themselves as a source of joy to their parents—says Dr. Richard A. Warshak in *The Custody Revolution: The Father Factor and the Motherhood Mystique*. "Grandparents who take obvious delight in their grandchildren offer a priceless antidote to such deprivation. Also, grandparents who remain available to the children provide a safe haven from the hostilities and offer a valuable sense of stability" (p. 66).

While most of life's roles take planning, the important role of grandparent simply happens to you. Grandparenting experts agree the grandparent-grandchild bond is second in emotional power only to the parent-child relationship. Because many grandparents are free of the disciplinarian role, they can offer a relaxed atmosphere of acceptance to their grandchildren. The well-known pediatrician T. Berry Brazelton has said, "Grandparents show children the mountaintops, while parents must teach them the drudgeries of how to get there."

As Dr. Mary Cerney, a psychologist and psychoanalyst at the Menninger Clinic, puts it: "Grandchildren and grandparents can fulfill a powerful need in each other to be listened to, to have one's thoughts and ideas taken seriously, and to be cherished with few, if any demands placed upon each other except to be."

In this chapter, we will look at the grandparent-grandchild relationship, focusing on how you can establish or maintain a strong relationship whether you live close to your grandchildren or far away, and how you can use this relationship to help them cope with the divorce and its aftermath. We will also consider how you can assist your grandchildren indirectly by building bridges with the other side of the family, that is, the other set of grandparents and, in most cases, the noncustodial parent. When you adopt and promote a positive and forgiving attitude, you can go a long way toward healing the wounds of divorce.

THE GRANDMOTHER-GRANDCHILD RELATIONSHIP

Very few women of today fit the traditional grandmother stereotype. Most are active in a variety of occupations and/or volunteer interests outside the home. Research indicates that these women tend to see their grandmother-grandchild relationships as qualitatively different from those they remember from their own childhood. They say they understand grandchildren's needs and emotions better than did their own grandmothers. And they are more likely to see themselves as warm friends for grandchildren, as people who provide special nurturing, and as role models—rather than as mother substitutes, baby-sitters, or caretakers.

In interviews, the majority of grandmothers say they love this role and take delight in seeing their grandchildren. As one grand-mother remarked, "How can you measure the thrill you feel when a grandchild runs to greet you exclaiming 'Grandma'?"

Being a grandmother gives a woman a second chance. She can enjoy her grandchildren in ways that were not as easy with her own children. Back then, she had the responsibility and day-to-day challenges of their care.

Nevertheless, grandmothers are committed to helping with child care *if it's on an occasional basis*. They are available in case of illness or other emergency and to relieve the parent of this re-sponsibility from time to time. Some grandmothers help with afterschool care, but since we're seeing more and more working grandmothers, lending this type of assistance is less common than in the past. (See chapter 4 if you have trouble setting limits on child care.)

Whether they're picking up their grandchildren at the school-house door, schlepping them to basketball practice, having them over for dinner or the weekend, grandmothers are pitching in with hands-on help. In single-parent families, such help is sorely needed. As one grandmother says: "My daughter and the children have their own place now. But with her long hours at work, and no second parent around, these kids would be with sitters all the time if we [grandparents] weren't around." And another: "They were going down the tube, the kids I mean. There was no continuity, no stability. Suddenly, I feel as if I'm doing something important with my life. As a concerned grandparent, I see that I can make a differ-ence in the life of another human being."

Helping out in the nineties is as likely to include taking in food or going out to a restaurant as cooking meals for the family. Says one grandmother, who hates to cook: "I want to help my son and his children. So I have them all over for Sunday dinner, and we have Chinese or Italian food delivered. They don't seem to care that Grandma didn't cook it as long as we're all together as a family."

The activities that grandmothers and grandchildren enjoy together are much more varied than they used to be. (See the section on hands-on activities later in this chapter.) One grandmother shares a popular activity with her grandson that no one had even heard of until a few years ago: "A grandmother on Rollerblades? Yep, that's me! When my grandson and his mom came home to live with us, and then at their own place, my grandson moaned as to how he used to Rollerblade with his dad. . . . I bought myself a pair of Rollerblades, and now he and I go Rollerblading. I've even lost weight!"

With no rigidly defined roles for the grandmother in a single-parent family, she knows she needs to be flexible. Yet she never wavers from her commitment to being a true benefactor and friend to her grandchildren. She is their beacon of hope, who not only promises that life will get better but actually takes action to see that it does.

THE GRANDFATHER-GRANDCHILD RELATIONSHIP

Today's new breed of grandfather may be observed dictating grandfatherly notes via fax machine to grandchildren who live out of town, coaching a soccer or Little League team for a granddaughter or a grandson, "working out" with weights alongside a grandchild, doing laps in the pool next to a ponytailed five-year-old granddaughter who can easily outswim him, attending basketball or hockey games with a grandchild or two, going camping or on nature walks. He also attends PTA meetings (for a grandchild) and in general acts as a stand-in for an absentee dad or mom. And he does all of the above not so much out of obligation or duty but in an amiable, warmhearted manner.

One grandfather, in a revealing statement, explains how he felt about rising to meet the challenge of grandparenting when his grandchildren moved home with him and his wife for several months.

There aren't many challenges left for a guy like me. I'm about to retire soon. But I see a challenge in grandparenting. I'm giving these kids as much love and time as I can manage, and after my retirement, I intend to do a heck of a lot more with them. Not just because it's the right thing to do and they need a man in their life, but because it's fun. Being with my grandchildren makes me feel young! Strange but nice thing about life: My granddad thought I was the most special person in the world. We really had a close relationship. Did a lot together. And here I am passing on what was given to me!

Another grandfather reports: "I used to get high on achieving and accomplishing in my career—work being my 'elixir.' Now my grandchildren are the substance of life that energizes me—fulfills me."

It is heartening to see that today's grandfather is no longer just an interested bystander or a financial provider. Society has given him permission to be a friend and caretaker who is actively involved in the lives of his grandchildren. Witness the following remarks: "Boys need the intimacy of wrestling or roughhousing with a dad, or if not a dad, someone like me, a granddad. . . . So when my grandson comes to visit on Sunday or stays overnight with us, I get down on the floor with him. He loves it, and, you know, so do I." A wife states that her husband is a " 'made for TV' grandpa! He . . . plays with [the grandchildren], will fix them a light supper, and even supervises the baths, if they stay over. He's retired now, and I think he's making up for all the time missed when our own little girls were growing up."

The grandfather-grandchild bond is one of mutual appreciation. One young grandson gives the following assessment of his grandfather: "Poppy is a cool guy. He doesn't mind when I ask him questions when the football game is on. And I know he really doesn't like hockey, but he'll watch it with me anyway. And sometimes when my mom's boyfriend can't take me to a hockey game, Poppy will." Another grandchild poignantly observes that a grandfather can "sort of replace a father while you don't have one around."

Poppy, Gramps, or Pop-Pop is a guy to look up to. He's someone who can lend advice, if asked, but more important, he's someone you can count on, a pal to have fun with—creating a special bond that a grandchild treasures for a lifetime. It's a legacy that can be passed from this generation to the grandchild's generation and beyond.

HANDS-ON ACTIVITIES: WHEN YOU LIVE NEARBY

If you live near your grandchildren and they attend school, you may decide to watch them—at your home or theirs—from the time school lets out until their mother, or the custodial parent, returns from work. This arrangement avoids much of the loneliness and vulnerability experienced by "latchkey" children.

Because of your job, your health, or the number of grandchildren involved, you may need to find someone to assist you with after-school care. Consider hiring a teenage baby-sitter. If you can't manage to look after the kids each day of the week after school, perhaps you can work out an arrangement whereby you alternate days with this sitter.

Be sure to let the teacher and principal know who you are and about your involvement with your grandchildren. (Usually the custodial parent must send a note or in person vouch for who you are and give permission for you to pick up your grandchildren at school.) And find out if you can take the place of the parent at school conferences or plays or trips, if the parent is working and cannot attend.

Even if you don't get involved with after-school care, you'll probably be keeping your grandchildren at your home from time to time. Once a month, have them stay overnight for a weekend or one evening on a weekend so that the single, custodial parent can have a respite from child care in addition to beginning a new social life. Occasionally, try to keep one grandchild at a time—if possible overnight. It's a great way to bond, and the kids thrive on the one-on-one.

For last-minute decisions about "sleeping over," I keep a pair of pajamas and a set of underwear and a few pieces of clothing for each of my grandchildren. Plus an old jacket with a hood, if the weather suddenly changes; and bathing suits for the sprinkler. Each child also has a plastic cup with his or her name on it.

Try to develop some friendships with children your grandchildren's ages in your own neighborhood. If your grandchildren can play with these children, it takes a lot of the pressure off you to entertain them. (I have found that my own grandchildren sometimes like to play with the neighborhood children, but at other times, they want to be alone with me. So mix it up!)

What can you *do* when you spend time alone with your grandchildren? The trick is to "keep 'em busy!" Here are some suggested activities:

֍ Check with your town or city about signing up your grandchild for after-school soccer leagues or other activities.

֍ Your local YMCA or YWCA may have programs you can take advantage of. (Also parenting courses, if you think you need a refresher.)

֍ Local parks and city recreation departments usually have free summer programs for all ages.

֍ Local museums often have programs for children in the summer as well as throughout the year. Check them out.

❧ Local high schools have football, baseball, and soccer practices and games on their grounds (or at a nearby field). Take the children to watch for a while.

❧ Younger children love to go to a park to play ball, have a picnic snack, go on the slides, the swings, mix with other children. Bring along some boxed drinks, crackers, and tissues. If you keep in the back of your car a bouncy rubber ball and an old blanket to spread out on the ground, you'll be ready for impromptu trips.

❧ Kids love to bake and cook. Even young children can handle cookie and cake mixes, as well as preparing hamburgers, tuna salad, and pizza mixes.

❧ A lemonade stand is fun (but requires adult supervision if the children are very young).

❧ Many children like household projects. My eight-year-old grandson helps me clean and reorganize the pantry, and my five-year-old granddaughter smiles nonstop as she washes windows.

❧ Car washing in the warmer-weather months seems to delight all ages.

❧ Children love to water plants, and if you have the room, let them help plant a garden with you (and assist in weed pulling as part of the deal!).

❧ Save your old clothes and accessories so young grandchildren can play "dress-up."

❧ The local library is a wonderful resource for fun and learning. Children love having their own library card. Go often and get them in the habit of reading books. (Younger children can look through picture books.) Keep them posted about due dates and the necessity of caring properly for books. Many libraries have story times for younger children.

§ Little children love *laps*, tender embraces, and a little cuddling. Some quiet reading is always appreciated.

§ Invest in some building blocks—boys and girls love them. They also enjoy Lincoln Logs, Legos, and other building materials.

§ Save unusual boxes, if you have room. My grandchildren combine them with blocks and build all kinds of interesting-looking "futuristic" cities, airports, and skyscrapers.

§ Make pen-and-pencil holders out of old cans of frozen juices. They can be covered with paper and decorated with scraps of material.

§ Sewing projects are fun for all ages. Consider making rag dolls, puppets, or pillows. Collect scraps of material and trimming, and save ribbons and buttons, so you're well prepared.

§ Brown lunch bags, yarn, string, and paint can be made into puppets.

§ Children make wonderful "welcome" pictures for doors and walls.

§ Encourage your grandchildren to start—or add to—a collection. They can collect stamps, baseball cards, miniature cars and trucks (Matchbox is a popular brand), dolls and dollhouse furniture, rocks, seashells, etc.

§ Plan special activities for rainy days, "weepy" days, or sick days. Keep supplies in a hiding place, to be pulled out when needed. Invest in board games, jigsaw puzzles, Chinese checkers, regular checkers, playing cards, Old Maid, drawing paper, washable markers, crayons, children's scissors, tape, school-type paste, Play-Doh, bubble stuff, colored paper, coloring books, paint-with-water books, inexpensive paint sets and brushes, and lots of books to read.

❧ In a pinch, rent a video.

❧ In the summer, nothing beats running under the sprinkler. Buy a small, inexpensive plastic pool for little ones.

❧ Keep plastic bats and balls around. Go to a nearby playground or park if your yard is not big enough, and practice up for Little League or soccer.

❧ I purchased some secondhand tricycles and bicycles to keep in my outdoor shed; my grandchildren like to ride them when they come for a visit. Flea markets or garage sales can offer up some good finds on other kinds of equipment, too.

❧ When they are small, children like to visit the fire station, petting farms, and real farms. Some farms even have hayrides in the fall.

❧ Visit a local zoo, planetarium, or museum.

❧ Other enjoyable outings are to auto and boat shows, sports events, a children's show or concert, a local TV show, fairs, carnivals, and parades.

❧ Nature walks are good for the soul. Collect leaves, unusual stones, etc.

❧ Have the children make a bouquet for Mom or Dad.

❧ Clean up for a healthy planet—by going with you and picking up trash that people throw out of their cars or that is just lying on the ground. Bring trash bags for each kid, and make a game out of it and see who can find the most. (I give my grandchildren old gloves so they don't touch the trash.)

If you are worried that young grandchildren will make a mess as they work on indoor projects, buy a piece of plastic that is sold in fabric stores, and get one wide enough and long enough to put over your table. If you see the necessity, buy another piece of plastic for the floor. Or use newspaper or vinyl tablecloths (sold in dime-stores).

Instill in the grandchildren good cleaning-up habits. At our house, we explain that the rule is to "take out one thing at a time to play with; after you put it away, you may take out something else." It's helpful to keep a box of toys with the kids' names on top so they know where their things are at your house and where they are to go when they are through playing.

Be sure to remember that while your grandchildren will relish the time and attention you give to them, they will also appreciate a small gift from time to time. See the following section for some inexpensive gift ideas.

REACH OUT: WHEN THEY LIVE AWAY

Achieving a warm and satisfactory interaction between grandparent and grandchild is a far greater challenge when you are seeking closeness across many miles.

Defeating the obstacle of distance takes creativity. Yes, visits are vital. There is no replacement for face-to-face contact. But remember, visits will mean more if you keep in touch between times. Long-distance grandparenting can be fun and is essential if you want to build a relationship with your grandchildren.

One bright spot for long-distance grandparents: Therapists note that if visits are only occasional or for short periods, grandparents are likely to find it easier to ignore behavior that could be upsetting on an everyday basis.

Here are some distance-dissolving ideas to help bridge the miles:

❧ Go to see your grandchildren as often as you can. If you can't afford the plane fare, take a train or bus, or drive your own car.

❧ Bring goodies.

❧ Invite a grandchild(ren) to come and spend a weekend or a week (send the ticket, if needed—and if you can afford it).

❧ Send baked goods.

❧ Send or bring audio-video tapes of yourself (and spouse, if you have one).

❧ When you are visiting your grandchildren, assure them that you'll keep in touch by phone after you return home. Tell them they can call you collect if they need to talk. With a young grandchild, it may be helpful to tape your phone number to his or her dresser drawer (so it's always available), and you'll want to explain how to reverse the charges when calling collect.

❧ Routine telephone calls are especially important in the early stages of the separation or divorce. Try to call the child directly.

❧ Encourage correspondence at an early age. When you visit, bring envelopes and stamps, and preaddress the envelopes to yourself (postcards, too). Bring writing paper, pens, and pencils to leave with the grandchildren.

❧ Send postcards with pictures of the city you live in (or when you are on vacation). Familiarize your grandchildren with the area of the country you live in.

❧ Take a vacation (even a mini one) with one grandchild at a time, if possible. If not, take 'em all.

❧ Start a picture album, a family scrapbook, and send it to them (or bring it) and let them add to it.

❧ If you have an old camera (that works) or can buy an inexpensive one, send or bring it (with film) and exchange pictures often.

§ Children love getting mail addressed to them. Send a package of inexpensive items (jacks, crayons, paperback books, playing cards, etc.) (Once a month is a realistic time interval.) Letters are always welcome. Initially, faraway grandparents should try to write more often than once a month.

§ Get involved in your grandchildren's world—their school, their favorite activities, hobbies, etc. Ask about them.

§ Share with them a project *you* are working on; seek their help. If you collect recipes, for instance, they can cut some out from old magazines.

§ Start a family newsletter. Get other extended family to write a paragraph (make a chain out of it), or put their pictures in it.

§ Record the family history, and send each grandchild his or her own copy.

§ Read stories into a tape recorder, and send them to your grandchildren to listen to at bedtime or on long car trips.

§ Read *The Long-Distance Grandmother: How to Stay Close to Distant Children*, by Selma Wasserman.

Most long-distance grandparents send their grandchildren gifts through the mail. It's their way of showing that they care—even if they can't literally "be there" for the grandchildren on an everyday basis. When the grandchildren's parents divorce, grandparents typically want to step up the gift giving since they know that a present will cheer up a child who is hurting.

Gifts need not cost a lot of money. In her book *Simply Christmas*, Mary Thompson offers a variety of suggestions for creative and inexpensive gifts. (See also her chapter on "Gifts of Sharing and

Caring" for ways to help your divorced child and grandchildren through the holidays.) Some of these gifts include:

§ The perennial favorites: a bat and a ball, board games, jigsaw puzzles, comic books, magic tricks, playing cards, coloring books with crayons, art supplies (e.g., pencils, markers, or paint and white or colored paper), miniature cars, dolls, yo-yos, jacks, spinning tops, and so on.

§ Some items for a child's collection (of stamps, baseball cards, doll clothes, doll furniture, etc.). It's easy to send additional items on a regular basis.

§ Scraps of material and trimming (in a pretty box) for a child who sews. Add an inexpensive sewing kit to the package for a child who hasn't yet been introduced to this practical hobby.

§ Clothes and music tapes or CDs—especially good for teenagers if you're careful about making selections. This age group is very fussy.

§ A paperback book or books. See *The New York Times Parent's Guide to the Best Books for Children* by Eden Ross Lipton for suggested titles.

§ A subscription to a children's magazine. (Your grandchild will remember you each time an issue arrives.) A few favorites are *Ranger Rick* (published by the National Wildlife Federation), *Sports Illustrated for Kids*, *Children's Digest*, *Sesame Street* (for preschoolers), and *Seventeen* and *Teen* (for older grandchildren).

§ Items from such mail-order catalogs as Hearth Song (children's baking utensils, cookbooks, puzzles, etc.; phone 1-800-325-2502) and Childcraft (toys, puzzles, etc.; phone 1-800-631-5657).

COMMUNICATION TIPS FOR HELPING THE GRANDCHILDREN DEAL WITH THE DIVORCE

Whether you live near your grandchildren or far away, it's very important to keep up your ties with them despite the feud between their parents. A patient, nurturing grandparent can reduce the emotional impact of the divorce. Here are some tips on what to say and what attitudes to adopt:

⚜ Stay neutral as best you can to maintain the invaluable emotional security you can give your grandchildren. By being neutral, you can allow yourself, as your grandchild must, to have two relationships without feeling disloyal. *If the children ask, you can state your opinion of the situation.*

⚜ Lovingly listen to your grandchildren with an impartial ear as they tell you their feelings about their parents' divorce. Just listen. You don't have to question them, or tell them the negative feelings you may have about the way their parents are behaving.

⚜ Remember, your grandchildren are going through a difficult emotional time. It is your support and love, not your advice, that are most helpful.

⚜ Emphasize both parents' good qualities, rather than their bad, and avoid emphasizing the separation.

⚜ It helps the child to know that his parents loved each other when they decided to have him, even if they don't love each other now. (Say this only if you know it to be true.)

⚜ If you know this to be true, tell your grandchild that "a lot of children worry they caused their parents' divorce. In no way did you cause the divorce."

⚜ Help your grandchild deal with reality. If you know this to be true, you can state that "your parents are *not* getting back together."

❧ Talk about the diversity of today's families. (There are single-parent families, two-parent families, foster families, grandparent-grandchildren families, etc.) Explain that there is no *one* way to be a family. Reassure your grandchild, he or she is still very much a part of a family.

❧ The youngest of grandchildren need reassurance, nurturance, and stability, and lots of hugging. They feel totally abandoned and fear being homeless. Grandparents can provide all of the above.

❧ Slightly older children need grandparents, too, to be there to accept their feelings.

❧ Use the *displacement* technique (discussed below) when children are resistant to discussing sensitive issues.

Displacement is a means of talking with a child about painful issues and provides that child a *safe* way to share feelings in a "one step removed" fashion. It helps build a bridge of *trust* between adults and children. It is *accepting*. *It works*. (However, displacement takes time, patience, and repetition. It probably won't work the first time you try.)

To practice this technique, you phrase your statements in the "third-person invisible." In other words, you use generalized statements about "those other kids" and "their" experiences and feelings—to help your grandchild explore his or her *own* thoughts and feelings. For example: "I was reading that kids have a lot of angry feelings about divorce. Even twelve- or thirteen-year-olds have those feelings." Another example: "I've heard that sometimes guys are so angry that they take it out on the people closest to them, like moms."

BUILD BRIDGES WITH THE
OTHER SIDE OF THE FAMILY

For the common good of our grandchildren, we must find ways to join forces with the other side. We must try to rise above problems that are simply minutiae or that are based on spitefulness. When all the adults work together to "shore up" the grandchildren rather than allowing petty differences to widen the gulf, a fragmented family becomes less vulnerable to emotional insecurities.

Earlier in this book, I mentioned the word "mensch." A mensch rises above the pettiness of the moment in order to maximize family for the grandchildren. To be a mensch, you may have to transcend the entrenched attitudes of others. You may even be scoffed at by the other side, reveal some grandparents. One grandmother said that "a thick skin is a gift from God," as she waded through the fury of the other side. What is important here is to see "the big picture" instead of merely snapshots.

Family therapist Marc Rabinowitz asks, "Why alienate the other side? Why be enemies? Will this help your grandchildren? A resounding *no*! It's so easy to demean the other side. Yet nothing is to be gained. It accomplishes nothing." He reminds us of an old Chinese proverb: "Those who seek revenge should dig two graves."

Rabinowitz asserts that instead of maligning the other side, we grandparents ought to "establish a line of communication. Even minimal contact can ultimately help your grandchildren. Be respectful and polite."

And cultivate a forgiving attitude. Says Rabinowitz:

Part of the healing process is for the grandparent to see things more objectively—that what we seek is forgiveness on all sides—to move past this. Even though people in a family don't get along, they have to have a relationship for the welfare of the grandchildren. Grandparents shouldn't "burn any bridges" if at all possible. They should try to keep a relationship with the other side going. It's difficult to do at first—the hurt is so great. And, too, your child may see you as an enemy if you try to make overtures to the other side fairly early on in the beginning stages of the breakup. But as long as it is all right with your son or daughter, it should be okay to keep a dialogue going with the ex-daughter-in-law or ex-son-in-law or the other grandparents.

Other professionals also exhort us to foster a relationship with the other side, albeit a limited one. Be a consensus builder, they advise, instead of denigrating the in-laws, which doesn't serve the best interests of your grandchildren.

In *The Dance of Anger*, Harriett Goldhor Lerner claims that "children need to discover their own truths about family members by navigating their own relationships." So avoid making negative remarks to children, or in front of children, about the other side. That means no pejorative, belittling, or snide comments. And no whispering to your spouse "about them" or speaking in barbed jest. Children are uncanny about understanding caustic, sarcastic, or cynical remarks, even at an early age. They are also very savvy about picking up on every nuance—not only by the way in which you speak but even by your body language. They can thus see and hear what you think and feel.

If the other side chooses to act "small" or spiteful, you as a grandparent must call upon your inner resolve to ignore this negative behavior and do whatever it takes to look the other way. This is building bridges (not roadblocks) and being a mensch!

The Other Set of Grandparents

Divisiveness between the two sets of grandparents chips away at, or does not allow, the buttressing of a family. But when we work in tandem with the other grandparents, we open the floodgates of additional love and security for the grandchildren. Admittedly, one set of grandparents, more likely the parents of the noncustodial parent, may not fully appreciate what you deem as a "summons to duty." Yet exerting pressure on them offers little hope, as shown in interviews with grandparents who have tried this approach.

Sally Brush of the Aring Institute gives this advice:

> *If the mother is the custodial parent, perhaps the maternal grandparents can take the initiative. They can put out the* welcome *mat for the other grandparents. If you can talk to the other grandparents, try to get this point across: Can they appreciate how much richer the children would be with more grandparenting? . . . If there is the slightest show of interest from them, and they respond to your overtures positively—grab the opportunity!*
>
> *Of course, it goes without saying, the maternal grandparents in this instance should run all of this by the mother firsthand, before reaching out to the other grandparents. Your attitude should be open and honest with the grandchildren. If you can't get over your feelings, at least admit to them. "Even though I don't have a relationship with your other grandparents, I think it's important that you do—and I won't love you any less for having it!"*

Here are some suggestions from Brush on how to reach out to the other side:

§ If you live in the same city with the other grandparents, invite them to a play at school or a family picnic or a family gathering.

§ If the other grandparents live out of town, send a monthly box of school pictures or projects by the grandchildren and copies of their report cards and teacher comments.

§ Send recent photos and notes describing the funny things the grandchildren say and do. Do this on a regular basis. If you have the time, you can make up a newsletter with their pictures and phrases.

Brush advocates keeping up these gestures *even* if you don't receive a response. "It's all a part of a much needed *open-door policy*," she claims.

Studies show that noncustodial grandparents can become more distant, but this is not an absolute rule, claims Dr. Arthur Kornhaber. While Kornhaber adds that quite often "the noncustodial grandparent is in danger of being displaced," others in the mental health field say it does not necessarily have to be so.

Most professionals agree that it is not wise to make a big deal about it if the other grandparents are not forthcoming or active with the grandchildren. To avoid any further rejection for these grandchildren, they suggest there is a need for the custodial parent to allow the disengaged or distant grandparent a degree of choice or a degree of spontaneity of involvement. Let them come on their own volition, advise several mental health specialists. And maintain a neutral attitude so as not to jeopardize any meaningful relationship between the grandchildren and these other grandparents at some time in the future. It is highly probable, they assert, that disengaged grandparents will eventually have a conversion of sorts and be more concerned and involved with their grandchildren.

A divorced mother told me she would have welcomed more help from her former husband's parents, but it was not forthcoming. "Perhaps I didn't do enough in asking them to do things with or for the kids. Probably if I had asked, they would have done more. My message to other divorced parents is: *don't be afraid to ask*. When I promoted an outing or a visit, they went for it and seemed to enjoy it."

"Grandparents can be like an oasis in a sea of controversy," says Judge Joanne Alper, of the Juvenile and Domestic Relations Court of Arlington, Virginia. Witness how the following grandparents encouraged a relationship between their grandchildren and the grandparents from the other side of the family:

The divorce was still very fresh. The air was thick with hate and getting even. I called my daughter long distance one day and asked what the grandchildren were up to. She said they were supposed to attend the circus with their paternal grandparents. "But," she declared, "I'm not letting them go. My ex-husband is insulting on the phone, and whenever I call there and his parents answer, they are cold and nasty. Why should I let them have the pleasure of their grandchildren? They haven't been the least supportive of my situation!" When my daughter and I talked about who she was really punishing, she came to her senses. Parents, unfortunately, especially in the beginning stages of the divorce, will use the children like pawns in a chess game.

When our daughter and grandchildren lived with us, the paternal grandparents, who lived in another state, became more and more distant and removed from the grandchildren's lives. (We never could understand this, since the grandchildren had lived for four years in the same city with them!) We would dial the phone for the little ones so they could speak to their other grandparents. And we encouraged them to write their other grandparents. And we would help them get started so this would develop into a weekly habit.

We also told these other grandparents that any time they were near our community, they were welcome to see the grandchildren and could take them for the day. (Of course, we had to clear this with their mother—our daughter.)

At first, they seemed stunned by the gesture—it threw them. They probably thought we were angry at them because their son caused the divorce. But we didn't or don't even now, feel that grandparents should lose out on being close to their grandchildren, just because their son messed up!

The Other Parent

From both the legal and medical fields, we are asked to keep in mind that it is incumbent upon grandparents to understand that access to their own grandchildren depends to a degree upon the quality of their relationship to the child's parents, and in a broken marriage, to the child's custodial parent.

If the custodial parent is your former daughter-in-law or son-in-law, you'll have to be especially careful. The pervasive anger that persists even after the divorce is final can easily infect your relationship with this individual. And if you alienate the custodial parent, you may be in danger of losing grandparental visitation rights.

Court records are replete with stories of how grandparents cause problems for grandchildren and, therefore, are unable to act in the best interest of their grandchildren.

In one case, a custodial parent (the mother) was continually maligned by one of the paternal grandparents in front of the granddaughter. As a result, when she would return from a visit with this grandparent, the girl became verbally abusive and at times incorrigible toward her mother. When these actions continued unabated, the court ordered no further paternal grandparent visitation. Mediation and therapy for the grandparent was ordered by the judge, and only when this negative attitude and behavior had ceased was visitation resumed. Initially the visitation was limited and in the presence of the mother. Eventually, however, the child was allowed to visit with the grandparent alone, after monitoring by social services.

Promoting a healthy relationship between the custodial parent and child, including the best-interest-of-the-child doctrine, is a judicial philosophy recognized in every court in this country. (Further illustrations of legal access to grandchildren and denial of same are presented in chapter 6.)

If your former son-in-law or daughter-in-law is the noncustodial parent, it's still important to have a civil relationship—for the sake of the grandchildren. One set of grandparents extended a very generous offer:

> *Our former son-in-law lives far away. We realize how difficult it is for him to live on what he earns, pay child support, and still have funds with which to fly here and see his children. So from time to time we have offered our home and our car (this would save hotel room and car rental). And so he wouldn't have to face us (he is still embarrassed and guilty about the cause of the divorce), we even offer to not be here when he comes and not return until after he has left. So far, he has not taken us up on our idea. Pride, I guess, but foolish pride at best. If he took us up on our offer, he could see his children more often!*

WHAT TO SAY (AND WHAT NOT TO SAY) TO YOUR ADULT CHILD

As we discussed in chapters 1 and 2, you can be a tremendous source of emotional support for your newly divorced child. You'll accomplish the most if you know what to say (and what not to say). The important thing, states divorce specialist Bonnie Winters, is not to take sides, and to avoid recrimination. She recommends that you

> *Don't say things like, "Why did you marry him?" or "I told you so," etc. The "whys" just don't help anyone! Divorce becomes overwhelming. It is so much better for your adult child if you remain nonadversarial. Try not to exacerbate existing hostilities between the two families. And cool the rhetoric about the in-laws (whom you probably never liked, anyway!) at least for the children's sake.*
>
> *New single parents . . . are often starved for affection them-selves—not just the grandchildren. Sometimes they need cheerlead-*

ers! *Praise their efforts as much as possible. The divorcing child needs a few "rah-rahs" for what he or she is trying to accomplish. Focus on the positive.*

Winters believes strongly that parents can set the tone for how the adult child (and grandchildren) will go about making their adjustment. "Tell the adult child, 'Forgive yourself. We all make mistakes in judgment. You had no way of knowing,'" suggests Winters. Other supportive remarks include: "I know you can get through this"; "I know you have the inner resources to be a strong person"; and "Remember, you have family—you have us."

Some additional advice from Winters:

The grandchildren are more than likely grieving, too, and acting it out, as well. Children usually take out their fears and frustrations, anger and resentment on the person they feel the safest with. Ask, "Are you feeling overwhelmed, dear, with the children? What can we do to help?" These types of questions will be more caressing and healing than jumping in with advice or taking over.

And try not to feed into their fears. It's scary for a newly divorced adult child to suddenly find themselves with all the responsibilities of child care, which was once a joint venture with their mate. Avoid remarks like, "Oh, I wouldn't want to be a single parent," or "I couldn't do what you're doing!" While you can acknowledge the situation with "I'm so sorry you have to go through this," follow up with a positive, "you've got the gumption to do this" style of remark to bolster their courage.

4.
The
Path to Relief

§

Most of us have been there before. We know the words and antici-
pate the action. It's time for takeoff. The stewardess reminds us to
buckle up. She mentions the possible loss of cabin pressure and
how the oxygen mask will pop out from the overhead compartment
if needed. At the end of her spiel, she admonishes us to clasp the
mask over our own nose and mouth before attempting to assist our
child.

And so it is that we grandparents must find our own path to
relief before we can try to relieve the pain of our adult child and
grandchildren. If we do not attend to our pain and become whole,
what can we accomplish for the good of this beleaguered family?

"We don't always have the luxury of separating our pain from
the pain of our divorcing daughter or son. So often we try to do
everything at once," observes Marc Rabinowitz.

Don't expect too much from yourself during this stressful time.
Be patient with yourself, and give yourself time to heal. You should

let yourself feel the pain. It is proof that you're alive! By doing this, you will get through the grieving process faster and will feel better.

"Writing in a journal about what you are feeling is an excellent release," says Jane Kaminski. "It's cathartic for you as a grandparent going through your pain. The point is that to be able to listen to your feelings and to write them, you can often come to understand them."

Listen to your body. It needs rest. Your body needs energy to repair. Pay attention to diet, and eat well. Mild exercise (e.g., walking) and the use of relaxation tapes can be helpful. Divorce specialists at the Aring Institute offer the following advice: Keep decision making to a minimum. Judgment is clouded when people are under stress. Surround yourself with things that are alive, such as plants, fish, and flowers. Be sure to schedule activities for weekends and holidays. These are difficult times during grieving periods. By preparing for them ahead of time, you'll be better able to handle those extra hours. If mementos of your child's wedding bind you painfully to the past, hide them or get rid of them. *But remember the grandchildren's pictures. Keep those baby photos proudly on display, even if the wedding albums go into hiding.*

Work to build a team of support: friends, family, ministers, parents, counselors, and—if you are lucky enough to have a spouse—your mate. Lastly, admit that the act of forgiveness is significant in returning to any degree of normalcy.

SETTING LIMITS: KNOW WHEN AND HOW TO SAY NO

At the beginning of the crisis, your life may very well be constantly interrupted with emotional and contradictory phone calls from your son or daughter. How should you react to these calls, and should you set limits on frequent phoning? According to Marc Rabinowitz:

It's actually reassuring to set limits during a crisis. When someone is in therapy, we work with them on structure—on balancing their lives. It is not useful to go on "ad nauseam." One needs organization—not compulsive responding. If there is someone who calls around the clock, we work with them on trying to write down what they are thinking about. The goal is to try and manage it themselves—to provide structure. Limit setting on phoning you by your recently divorced child is OK. But of course, in the first week, ten days, or two weeks—in the midst of the crisis, everything's fresh— the breakup—it's all right for the frequent phoning. After that, get on with it. Make plans. Set times and frequency of calls, if possible.

Unfortunately, too many grandparents admit to succumbing to "parent-by-phone" hysteria. This "phoning frenzy" (mostly in long-distance situations) usually takes place in the wake of the initial separation. Mental health specialists say we should be wary of necessarily acting upon what we hear over the telephone in the immediacy of the breakup. These excessive telephone communiqués, motivated by feelings of fear, anger, and frustration, are related to our adult child's sense of losing control over his or her life.

Too many parents misconstrue the pushing of emotional hot buttons as an invitation to jump in and make decisions for their adult child. But remember that in the heat of the crisis, decision making can be skewed—and that is not in the best interests of your adult child, your grandchildren, or yourself.

Our incessant quest for instant solutions does not serve us well. We offer up ready-made, quick-fix answers to problems our adult children are experiencing without regard to letting things settle down. Emotions that are ladened with anger, hurt, and sadness will begin to dissipate with time.

We would do better, say the experts, to act as a sounding board and offer our good ear in those early days. Our adult children need time to unravel what has happened and to *reason themselves* out of their dilemma. We are advised to be a low-level guiding force, rather than the preeminent one, when decisions are discussed. Be discerning with your advice giving, they advocate, when everyone is out of equilibrium.

The ebb and flow of telephone ideas and plans by your son or daughter will astound you. As one grandparent candidly related: "During the initial separation, our daughter would call us five and six times a day—each time with a different agenda. First she was coming home with the kids; then she would call within hours, to say just the opposite. We soon realized she was just thinking out loud and needed the sound of our voices as reassurance more than as decision makers. By the third or fourth week—after the shock waves wore off—her common sense surfaced. She just needed time to gather in her instincts and get her bearings."

Another grandmother said that she and her husband were unable to get any sleep those first weeks. Their son was extremely depressed about his wife's leaving. He was an active father. Now he could see his children only on weekends. He was lonely. These grandparents were fearful for the emotional health of their son; they worried he might even commit suicide. So when he would call them in the middle of the night "just to talk," they would listen and try to lift his spirits. With time, the calls lessened and he did adjust and adapt. But to this day, these grandparents recall vividly how exhausted they were from lack of sleep and how hard it was to function productively at their respective jobs. Yet although the grandfather told me that " 'I must get some sleep' was a sentence at the tip of my tongue whenever our son would call at three or four in the morning . . . because of his sensitive nature and the pain we knew he was experiencing, we just couldn't say it. Perhaps, if the divorce had been less traumatic—less of a shock—maybe we could have done it."

Jennette Franklin, a social worker, has spent countless hours with besieged grandparents, helping them in setting limits on their time, energy, and resources. "In some instances, I see the adult child hasn't come to grips with or come to the life stage of realizing that his or her parents are never going to be these all-nurturing, all-wonderful, 'always there for them' people. If these adult children haven't come to terms with this fact before the divorce occurred, then they are still so needy—still grabbing. Their pain and immaturity are so demanding—so sucking. They switch over from trying to get everything from their spouse to going back to trying to get everything from these parents."

"When the parents of adult children going through the divorce are consumed, it makes me wonder about whether there is a large enough separation between that parent and child," notes Marc Rabinowitz.

According to Franklin, "It's so difficult for people going through divorce to get back that feeling of 'I am lovable. This person that I loved so long and so intensely doesn't love me anymore.' Then what happens in some cases is they try to get back this 'I'm still lovable, aren't I?' from the parents. There are so many variables in all of this. How old are these divorcing adult children? What was the duration of the marriage? Where are they in their maturing process? What is the state of their relationship to their parents?"

Jane Kaminski recommends that the custodial parent have a backup person if the grandparent cannot provide all the desired support (in case of poor health or a grandparent's work schedule, if the other spouse needs care, or if there are other demands on the grandparent's time). "The parents of these grandchildren should understand that the grandparents did not envision this responsibility at this stage in their life. The divorcing adult child should be aware of how this new responsibility impacts on his or her parent's life."

"Grandmothers are women who are so used to doing things for others, they often do not look out for themselves," warns Dr. Karen Lewis, a family therapist in Washington, D.C.

She says that when grandmothers try to be assertive and say "No, I don't want to do such and such," or "I can't do that today," they worry about not being considered a good grandmother. According to Dr. Lewis, "You need a clear description and definition of what it is your son or daughter is expecting of you. And in turn you must clarify and be definitive about what part of the plan, if any, you feel able and willing to do." Dr. Lewis further states that if you as grandmother feel you are being used too much, you must say so to your son or daughter—but in a cordial, nonangry way.

A working woman is likely to feel torn between her role in the workplace and her role as a grandmother. On the one hand, most of her time and energy are taken up by her job, and she cherishes the few free hours that she has. On the other hand, she wants to help her grandchildren and adult child as they adjust to their new way of life. Although some working grandmothers do not have trouble saying no to requests for baby-sitting (perhaps because they consider working to be a legitimate excuse), many others end up saying yes even when it's not convenient. Experts in the mental health field suggest that working grandmothers modify their values and beliefs about what grandmothering "ought" to be. Grandmothers will also feel better if they take it upon themselves to find—and perhaps pay for—a substitute who can tend to the grandchildren when the grandmother is unavailable.

Many grandmothers also feel that their adult children do not fully appreciate their dedication to their jobs or their involvement in other activities. Some say that their work is demeaned by their adult children as less worthwhile than caretaking a grandchild. Here again, being assertive and talking things out are the recommended ways to resolve the situation.

"There appears to be a lot of anguish when grandparents become assertive," says Marc Rabinowitz. " 'I can't do that' or 'We have to take care of ourselves'—assertive statements like these confuse grandparents. They think they are not being supportive of the family in need." Rabinowitz tells grandparents, "If you don't take care of yourself, you aren't much good to anyone else."

Rabinowitz speaks of clients who get in over their head. These grandparents, he says, promise to help out with the grandchildren when their daughter or son goes back to work. But often they cannot sustain their promise; child care becomes too much for them. Rabinowitz sees many adult children who are unable to accept the fact that their parents cannot handle this job—or understand that their parents are aging, they are tired, and they need more rest at this stage in their lives.

"I have to reinforce to this grandparent that you are not locked into anything," says Rabinowitz. He argues that we must renegotiate arrangements if they are too demanding on us. It is up to us to set the tenor and the tone, and to be clear about what we are comfortable doing as both parents and grandparents.

One grandmother describes her own difficult situation and how she went about turning it around:

> *At times I felt like a sinking ship. I was on a guilt trip, too, whenever I didn't help out. I had to see a therapist because I was overly involved with my grandchildren's care. Turned out I was also making my daughter too dependent on me. She was asking too much, and I didn't assert myself enough and say no. Practicing some assertive techniques and in joint sessions with the therapist and our daughter, our relationship improved. We had to learn about balance and setting parameters. She had to break the dependency cycle she had had with her husband, our former son-in-law, and now with me. I'm laying back a lot more and remembering who the real mom is supposed to be. And our daughter is assuming more responsibility for her children.*

FINDING HELP FOR YOURSELF

Coping with your pain requires talking it out. If you can talk with a spouse, all well and good. But if not, look to a friend. Maybe you have a friend who has been down that road before you—who made the journey but didn't get lost. If you can have a heart-to-heart talk on a regular basis with this friend, it can be a useful means of synthesizing your pain. The underlying premise is that you can learn from each other in the comforting and sharing of pain (in the so-called fellowship of suffering).

But sometimes our friends cannot give us the support that we need. As one couple explained: "None of our friends really understand. They may sympathize, but they don't really know what it's like or what we're going through or how to help us. They actually don't want to be involved, you can tell." These grandparents made the decision to join a support group. There they found a roomful of kindred souls with whom they could communicate.

Grandparent Support Groups

How do grandparents cope with their adult child's divorce? Would they have done anything differently if they had to do it over? How do they transcend their feelings toward the other side of the family for the benefit of their grandchildren? These are but a few of the questions that are discussed in grandparent support groups.

Sally Brush, director of Beech Acres' Aring Institute, discusses the grandparent support groups at her institution:

We concentrate on techniques for grandparents [many of which are listed in chapter 3] to assist them in becoming more adept at listening as opposed to "fishing" with both the grandchildren and the divorcing adult child. We try and help grandparents focus their energy toward their grandchildren and son or daughter and to channel their anger about the divorce elsewhere. Our grandparent support group addresses such issues as reconciling the limit setting of time, money, hands-on help, space, and even dreams!

The basic tenet in all of our divorce groups is "this is the most important business you'll ever be in—this divorced family of yours."

This approach has been adopted in our grandparent groups, as well. . . .

Acting as a facilitator in the grandparent support group, I let them talk with no set structure. Some grandparents don't speak out as much as others, but claim they still get a lot from the group.

Observes Jane Kaminski, in discussing the support group for grandparents that she leads: "Some members of my group want to share and share 'ad nauseam,' while others are less open about their problems or feelings. Yet even those reluctant members will still learn and benefit from the group just by listening. And eventually, many open up."

Kaminski's support group for grandparents initially is led by a professional. After it is in full swing, it is turned over to the group itself, with a facilitator. What is shared by the group stays within the group. The ground rule is confidentiality. It's important for everyone in the group to know that what they say does not go beyond that room, so they can vent their true feelings without fear of anyone else knowing. This is an opportunity to share, and everyone gets a chance to speak. "I try to make sure that no one person is pouring his or her heart out at the exclusion of the other members of the support group, or taking over," says Kaminski. She wants to imbue the group members with a mutual respect for one another and an understanding that some people are just more reticent about sharing their innermost thoughts.

"What I have noticed in my grandparent support group," says Kaminiski, "is that grandparents for the most part have very little perception of what it's like to be a working single parent. Most of them—the grandmothers—did not work outside the home when they were raising their children. On the other hand, I also find that the adult child of these parents can barely grasp the situation of what it is like to be a grandparent—to be closer to dying—to face feelings of retirement or the fear of being alone one day without their spouse." In their support of one another, members of the group can at least understand the *feelings*, if not the situation itself.

Support groups are a nonthreatening place where people can be heard. There appears to be a specific phenomenon that can happen in a group that cannot occur in individual therapy. There is this feeling of "I am not alone." Here you experience people who have been where you are, and it gives you hope to see others who are farther along the path to recovery than you are.

As each grandparent story unravels, contrasting views may emerge. Yet these same grandparents can allay one another's fears and identify with one another's hurts while divulging poignant memories of their own. Conflicted feelings evoke empathy and elicit candid revelations. Suddenly there is this commonality (never mind that the specifics in each story do not match). The goal, the bottom line, is quite simple: to strengthen the life of a grandchild going through his or her parents' divorce.

The following comments are from members of various support groups around the country:

From comforting each other, we have learned new ways to handle our family difficulties. And we are learning to accept what cannot be changed—to bend rather than crack.

We are trying to soften the impasse with our adult child and to be open-minded about her life-style and her way of parenting.

We discovered that many of our coping mechanisms were ineffective with these three-generational relationships. And, too, there are so many facets to this grandparent-grandchild bond nowadays that I had not realized existed.

Despite the considerable benefits of support groups, many grandparents are reluctant to join them. Sally Brush says: "I think we'd see more grandparents coming to support groups if they weren't so embarrassed about their son or daughter's divorce. As a result of their self-consciousness (along with feelings of failure as parents or role models), many do not seek out support groups as much as they could (or therapy, or clergy or talking it out)."

"Out of a traditional sense of responsibility, they, the grand-parents, do what is required of them. It is part of this generation's mode of thinking," suggests Marc Rabinowitz. "There is this sto-icism about them, which is why I think that many grandparents do not seek therapy for this situation. They are not open to complain-ing about what they see as something they must do. This is a com-mitted generation as a whole."

Divorce program specialist Bonnie Winters couldn't agree more. "There would be far more grandparent support groups across the country and more grandparents seeking counseling if people of this age group weren't so stoic. They just *do*, without questioning!"

Those who work in the people-helping fields believe that it's critical to get together with people who are in similar situations. In their view, support groups are so essential that they advise you to form an informal network or start your own support group if there are no grandparent support groups in your community.

You may wish to consider the following questions, offered by a variety of mental health specialists, when beginning your own sup-port group:

 ৬ *Where will you meet?* Libraries, hospitals, churches, and syna-gogues often will make a meeting room available. Nearby com-munity and/or recreation centers may also have a meeting room you can use.

 ৬ *Is the location accessible?* Can members easily make the drive or take a bus to meetings?

 ৬ *When will you meet?* Get a consensus among the group on whether to have meetings in the day or evening, and whether to hold them once a week, bimonthly, or monthly.

❧ *Should a baby-sitting service be available?* Many grandparents are involved in caretaking responsibilities.

❧ *What fee will you charge?* The fee should be on a sliding scale so that no one is denied access to the support group because of income.

❧ *Should you advertise in the newspaper?* If you take out an ad, remember that you do not necessarily have to list your own telephone number or address; you can use a box number. Instead of, or in addition to, an official advertisement, you might be able to give the details of your group (place, time, and purpose of the meeting) on a public-service-announcement page of your newspaper.

❧ *How else can you get the word out?* Put up a notice of the intention to form a group on bulletin boards in churches, supermarkets, recreation and/or community centers, tennis and swim clubs—just about any place where lots of people your age congregate. Also contact any agencies in your community that have senior citizen organizations.

YOU'RE IN A COUPLE? DON'T LOSE YOUR MARRIAGE, TOO

How do you maintain your marriage while tending to the needs of your adult child and grandchildren, which are immense in the beginning stages of the divorce? Grandmothers in particular feel they are being pulled in two directions as they become very involved with their grandchildren while attempting to honor their commitment to their spouse. Unfortunately, many adult children have to be sensitized to this "pull."

One grandmother spoke about her inability to keep up with the after-school care of her grandchildren, as she had originally promised, because her husband, the grandfather, had become ill. Jennette Franklin: "Adult children have to realize that with aging comes the possibility of . . . [such a situation]. There wasn't any choice for this grandmother of where her first duty was."

Another factor in this grandmother/grandfather role, admits Franklin, is the difference in approach between the two sexes. "Oftentimes, a grandfather is not involved to the degree that the grandmother wants him to be. I try to counsel the grandmother as to how and why he is reacting this way. Maybe he is making a contribution in a less direct way, I say, but no less a contribution to the adult child and grandchildren. And perhaps, as is often the case, he was not that involved with his own children and can't change the way he is."

Franklin indicates to the grandmother that in all likelihood, her husband is not going to assume the "classic" grandfather role. "I try to help her see that she needs to set limits so as to have time not only for herself, but to pay attention to and further her marriage to Grandpa!"

Family therapist Karen Lewis concludes that "the same things that Grandfather does not notice about you and your new involvement with your adult child and grandchildren, are probably the same things he did not notice when you had children." Lewis offers the following advice: "Talk to your husband. He may well be jealous of the time and energy you are now giving to your daughter or son and grandchildren. I tell grandmothers to speak to grandfathers in a way that translates thusly: 'If you want time with me or for me, plan it!' You see, the problem is grandmother needs to be given to, as she is doing so much giving at this juncture."

As things begin to settle down with your son or daughter (and the grandchildren), you need to start the weaning process. "Be protective of your privacy and your marriage, and take care of yourself," insists Franklin. "Don't lose yourself in all of this. Major stressors that come to us in life, like a divorce in the family, invariably destabilize a relationship like marriage. It's tough—it truly is a balancing act!"

Men, observe several mental health specialists with whom I spoke, do not know how to ask for more attention, because they are often out of touch with their own feelings. Grandmothers, they contend, can get so overextended in their new grandparental role that they are often physically and emotionally drained. So much so, that they don't take notice of the angst in their husbands.

Professionals also suggest that men's and women's socializing techniques are very different. Men, especially those in long-term marriages, look to their wives to maintain a social life with friends. The wife is usually the planner.

Frances Goldscheider, a sociology professor at Brandeis University and an editor of *Demography* magazine, suggests that "as men grow older, being part of a social network is more important than occupational success. And men's social lives have always been created by women."

Grandmothers confide to their therapists (and in interviews with me) that grandfathers can become morose and remote, if not outright angry and frustrated, at their sudden loss of companionship with Grandmother and their lack of privacy. Many grandfathers expressed being overwhelmed by this new responsibility with children and grandchildren. Some grandfathers became entrenched in solitude and admitted to being unable to verbalize or communicate their true feelings. When grandfathers are encouraged to talk it out with professional guidance, their insecurities are much abated, and the marital strain is eased.

"Men feel they're supposed to weather any storm without asking for support," notes North Carolina psychotherapist Chris Saade. Saade leads a group for men who want to explore the depth of their feelings. "Men don't have permission—cultural permission—to be in touch with their bodies or their emotions," suggests Saade.

But Saade and others say they're beginning to see changes, at least in the younger generation. "I think the sixties turned things around," says Dean Minton, a physician's assistant with the Center for Mental Health in Charlotte, North Carolina. "The women's liberation movement was one of the best things to happen to men." (We can only hope that older men will catch on, as well!)

Saade thinks that the men's movement has helped, too. "Men are starting to give each other support—to listen to what's happening inside them," he says.

Let's now listen to what a variety of grandparents have to say about how their lives—and especially their marriages—were affected by the divorce in the family:

When I'd come home on Fridays, after having spent the week on the road (I'm a traveling salesman), the only one that greeted me was the dog! My newly divorced daughter and the grandkids would be over from the time I arrived home on Friday. They'd be back again on Saturday and hang out at our place most of the day—and darned if they didn't turn up again on Sunday! Now don't get me wrong. I love that daughter of mine and those grandchildren, but I would have liked some private time with my wife. The only time we were alone was when we'd go to bed! One night at a friend's cocktail party, when I had had a bit too much imbibing, I let my wife know how I felt. She worked it out with our daughter. Now they get together a lot during the week while I'm on the road. I get to see the grandchildren and my daughter for a Saturday or a Sunday afternoon. Besides getting my wife back, I can have some needed privacy.

It was all-consuming—the phone calls, the letters. Soon I found myself unable to talk about anything else. My husband had his work at least. I was so totally enmeshed as to be practically disinterested in his comings and goings—his accomplishments or his worries.

Where I once prided myself on being neatly dressed and keeping up my clothes and hair, I began to have this "I don't care" attitude about my personal appearance. Soon after, I noticed a loss of sexual desire or interest on my part—for my husband.

Before he even got his coat off, the litany of worries about our newly divorced adult child and the grandchildren spewed forth in volcanic eruptions! It was like a compulsion disorder!

I couldn't sleep. It seemed as if as soon as I would lie down, my mind would be swirling with ideas about how to "fix" this thing—or how to ease the pain of my child and grandchild. My restlessness was disturbing my husband's sleep, so I moved into the guest bedroom. I developed insomnia. At three o'clock in the morning, there I'd be jotting things down in a notebook to tell my daughter!

We should have sought counseling from the beginning. It would have lifted the veil off our marriage. We both believe, looking back in hindsight, that this loss we felt—instead of bringing us closer— seemed to divide us. I needed to talk it out, and he just wanted to brood about it.

My husband's depression, frustration, and anger about our daughter's failed marriage, plus the worry over the instability in our grandchildren's lives and the financial drain—all combined to bring on my husband's temporary impotency.

I began to overeat—guess it was an outlet for what I was feeling— this inability to seemingly do anything constructive. But in time I learned to accept what I couldn't change and found ways to help my son and his children. The more meaningful things I did for the grandbabies gave me a lift. I felt I was making a difference. I saw that overeating was destructive and a negative outcome of the divorce. It sure wasn't helping them and certainly wasn't helping me to become and to remain an active grandmother!

We used to have more time together—especially on the weekends. My husband works all week. We would take drives down by the ocean or take long walks or catch a movie at the spur of the moment. Now I hardly have time for him. And I see a wall building up between us as he feels shut out. I'm working on explaining all of this to my daughter. Guess no matter how solid or how old a marriage is, it needs a continuing courtship.

I like to call my story "The Saturday Night Massacre!" My husband and I have always met friends or gone out by ourselves on Saturday. It's sort of a custom, I guess. Now my daughter is dating again, and sometimes she asked me to watch the children for a few hours on a Saturday afternoon while she went to the beauty parlor or did whatever she needed to do. (She works all week.) Well, I said "sure," at first. But when she didn't pick them up until four or four-thirty, I would be so tired out that I didn't enjoy myself in the evening. I wasn't "companion" material. I'd be dragging. So now, if I babysit on a Saturday afternoon, I set the hours to suit my schedule. I will only take them until three, so I can rest or fix my hair or get a manicure. I'm a better date now!

Whenever our grandchildren came to spend the night, I worried about the way in which we (my husband and I) communicated our minor disagreements. I was so sensitive to the fact of how my grandchildren heard their parents argue prior to the split. But I was told by my therapist: "As long as you're not drawing emotional blood, it's OK to have disagreements. It's natural—a part of life. Besides," she said, "it's a good lesson for children to take notice that a couple can resolve their difficulties and disagreements—they can work it out in a peaceful way." She reminded me that conflict resolution is part of living.

5.
"We're Coming Home"

§

WHEN THE

YOUNGER GENERATIONS

MOVE IN OR NEARBY

Two sisters lived in the same city. They were both in their late fifties—active, healthy, and with reasonable wherewithal. These were not their only similarities. Each sister was married, and each had three grown children (who were married and had families of their own). At approximately the same juncture in their lives, each sister faced the earth-shattering news that a divorced child was returning home (with little ones in tow!). But each handled the resulting changes in her life very differently, reinforcing the old adage that "attitude is everything in life."

Upon hearing of the impending return, the first "sister-grandmother" exclaimed: "Oh, my God. What a tragedy! My poor little girl and those babies! And my life . . . why it will never be the same! My private time, our space, my beautiful home," etc., etc. The other "sister-grandmother" had a very different reaction: "I never knew life could be so challenging and exciting!"

First comes perception, then comes attitude—so say therapists and family counselors. How you perceive things is quite often how they come to pass; it's a self-fulfilling prophecy. If you perceive a situation to be ripe with possibilities and wonder, then often these possibilities will indeed arise. But if you perceive a negative out-come, it is more than likely to be just that.

As Dr. Charles Parker notes, "One sister was comfortable with change. Obviously, the other was not. How we handle change and our ability to adapt and adjust to new patterns of living, difficult moments, and stressful relationships defines us to a degree." (In chapter 1, I discussed Dr. Parker's analogy about how the weeping willow—as opposed to the straight and erect tree—weathers a storm. We would all profit from applying this flexibility to our own lives.)

One of the best gifts we can give our children and grandchildren is to show them by example, by our attitudes and actions as mature human beings, that we have mastered the art of handling change and its challenge. We as grandparents can set the tone—to be the mentor in teaching this fledging family about life's sudden twists and turns and how to cope and manage the inherent conflicts that will surely arise.

The majority of grandparents I interviewed believe sincerely in what they are doing for their grandchildren and newly divorced daughter or son (or in some rare cases, their daughter-in-law or son-in-law). They take pride in fostering a more complete family life for a newly emerging, evolving family. They offer a "safe haven."

Nonetheless, in interview after interview, grandparents voiced the sentiment that knowing the situation is temporary, that there is a light at the end of the tunnel, makes it bearable. There is agreement among grandparents on the pitfalls that encompass their commitment. Fortunately, most of the dilemmas are negotiable and solvable—even if it sometimes requires the wisdom of a Solomon.

It may be useful for you to read about the discoveries made by a number of grandparents and the advice given by grandparents and experts alike. Grandparents use a variety of methods to cope with sibling rivalry, deal with great-grandparent conflicts, and tap into multilayered support systems. Unorthodox but effective ways are available to help one manage additional responsibilities while realistically reflecting one's own limitations. There are abundant paradoxes and ambivalences in the following case histories. But they shed the necessary light to illuminate hard realities and choices.

PAT'S STORY

Grandmother Pat tells what happened when her daughter Alyson and young grandson David came to live with her and her husband, Sheldon.

"When I first heard the news that . . . [they] were moving in with us, my first thought was, 'This is horrible.' At first, it was all-consuming, until we got into it more. Yet we were always aware of our loss of privacy. And I recall saying to my best friend, 'Oh, it's not my turn again, is it? Didn't I do this once before?'"

Dealing with Sibling Rivalry

Pat and Sheldon's other children were grown and out on their own. But they were still jealous of the increased attention paid to Alyson.

"I think back," says Pat, "at not having much energy, time, or focus for my *other* children whenever they would call long distance or come home for a visit."

Pat describes a birthday card she received from her youngest daughter, who was living several miles away. "The card showed an overgrown baby on the outside and inside my daughter had written 'Love, from your *real* baby'!"

"Whenever one sibling goes through a trauma, it affects the others," observes family therapist Marc Rabinowitz. Other therapists suggest that disruption in the family, by the return to the nest of a sibling with children of his or her own, even when the other siblings are not living in the home, can cause jealousy and envy. Professionals emphasize that although there may be a sound relationship between siblings and between you and your other children, the intensity of focus on the brother or sister with the immediate priority seems to cause hostilities.

Experts warn grandparents and parents to be careful not to alienate other family members by focusing too much attention on the sibling who has returned home. It's bad enough that they know expenditures of energy and dollars on behalf of a prodigal brother or sister may mean less for them.

A consensus will not emerge overnight. Siblings have competing interests, and no matter whether you try "to put the best possible face on it," as Pat did, a certain amount of tension will occur. How can we relieve or defuse some of these conflicts?

Dr. Karen Lewis, author and editor of *Siblings in Therapy*, advises parents not to ignore their other children. She emphasizes the need to make time to speak with them in an unhurried way. "Initiate the calls as often as you can," she suggests. "And if it's a long-distance relationship, visit as you did before, if at all possible."

Dr. Lewis further states that if siblings live in the same community, a parent or parents should provide a special time to be with each of them on a regular basis, even if it's for only an hour a week. "But be consistent," she says. "And if you can, let your sibling son or daughter choose the activity and place."

Helping a Daughter Get Back on Her Feet

"I think Alyson was extremely appreciative of the sacrifices we were making for her and David. She understood from the beginning that this was 'Mom's house and Mom's domain!' She did not intrude!"

When Alyson applied and was accepted into law school, receiving a partial scholarship, Pat and Sheldon agreed to back her emotionally, as well as financially.

Alyson did astonishingly well her first year, and I unabashedly take a good deal of the credit! Our daughter was able to concentrate and get off to a flying start, as I had grandson David in my care every afternoon after nursery school. And Sheldon and I did things with him on weekends so his mommy could study.

Once we became adjusted and developed a living style, accommodating each other's needs and space requirements, we were shocked when Alyson said she and David were moving into their own apartment. I didn't think she could do it—I mean, being in law school, studying so hard. And I was afraid of what it would do to David; he had just become adjusted to being with us. But Alyson felt the absence of what it was like to be the head of her own household as she had once been in the early days of her marriage, and I guess she apparently missed this. I had to overcome my fear of letting them go on their own.

Shortly after her divorce, Alyson had developed a relationship with a young man who later became her live-in boyfriend. With some financial help from the young man and a little stipend from Pat and Sheldon (with Alyson working part-time), everything seemed to fall into place.

Enlisting the Help of Great-grandmother

Pat did her best to perform her new responsibilities, especially for David's sake, but the job soon became a bit overwhelming. And Sheldon needed her at the office.

She used her resourcefulness to find a solution:

I enlisted the help of my mother, an active and feisty seventy-seven-year-old great-grandmother who worships and adores her great-grandson! Mother alternated with me so we each picked up David twice a week from nursery school and kept him at our respective homes two afternoons a week. And on the fifth day, we had a sitter take David to his own place [the new apartment] so he could get used to his own neighborhood and meet the boys and girls living near him. So it all worked, with lots of cooperation from many sides.

Ann, the great-grandmother, who lives in a high-rise building not far from where David lives with his mother and her live-in boyfriend, tells what she and David do when she has her "special" time with him: "Sometimes I take David to play with the video machines at a nearby 7-Eleven store. And other times we feed the ducks in the pond near my building. I'm an old 'flea market and garage sale' enthusiast, so I keep a good collection of old-fashioned toys around that most of today's kids never see. Besides, David and I are buddies! My family accuses me of never having grown up. Glad I didn't!"

A Grandson Thrives in Four Homes

According to Pat's assessment of the current situation, David is doing exceedingly well with the "chain of command." His support system is filled with people who genuinely care about him and with whom he interacts well. David's father has remarried, and his new wife has "connected" with David, remarks his grandmother. David spends every other weekend with his dad and his dad's new wife. Pat thinks that Alyson's live-in friend is a good influence, too, and a "constant" in David's life.

David's recent remark about his many homes points up the

adaptability of children when those that surround them are kind and caring and have a deep and abiding interest in their welfare. When asked where he lived when starting a new school, David boasted that he had four homes: (1) his mom's apartment, (2) his dad's apartment, (3) his grandmother and grandfather's house, and (4) "more" Grandma's place (his great-grandmother's apartment).

"Toys, books, secondhand bicycles and wagons, play clothes, and pajamas are kept at all four places. So David is 'always' home," concludes Pat.

There are, of course, bound to be differences between generations in parenting style. Pat alludes to what she views as lapses in child rearing or permissive attitudes by the actual parents. But she says, "I have learned to keep my mouth shut. David is happy, healthy, and doing well in school. He makes friends easily. What more can I ask for?"

MYRA'S STORY: UNDER ONE ROOF

"I always knew their marriage was in trouble," muses Myra, a divorced grandmother who works full-time. "It wasn't a good scene. And when the baby came, motherhood was very difficult for my daughter due to the turmoil in her life."

In speaking about her daughter, Ramona, and her grandchild, Emily, who both eventually moved in with her, Myra gets tears in her eyes.

I guess what goes around comes around. When I was divorced, I moved in with my mother and centered my life on my baby, just the way Ramona does now. Funny how history has a way of repeating itself in families.

The moving in? It was my idea, I guess. With a bare minimum of child support and no job, we just fell into a pattern that worked quite well. Since my daughter and I get along, that laid the ground-

work. Ramona took care of the apartment, the baby's laundry, and, of course, the baby.

I learned early on that letting Ramona make all the decisions about Emily would be the best. And I think my instincts were right on the money. Only if she asked me would I offer any suggestions.

Our major problem was my mother, Emily's great-grandmother, who was living with me at the time that my daughter and grandchild moved into the apartment. I was virtually a referee! With all four generations living together in one small apartment, the generation gap—especially between my mother, who was in her early eighties, and my daughter, who was twenty-two—presented a lot of hostility that made for uncomfortable living for everyone.

We tried, all of us, living together under one roof for about three or four months, but Mother was from the old school about how to care for a baby. My daughter could not accept her so-called suggestions. Funny thing, though, Ramona could take advice from me. But I think that's because we were always pretty close. I also did not suggest or advise or tell her what to do at every turn. My mother never stopped! I'd be at work, and each of them would call me, sometimes as often as three or four times a day, to complain about what the other one was not doing!

How did Myra, Ramona, baby Emily, and the great-grandmother solve their dilemma? Myra was the one who came up with a solution:

I knew that my daughter and baby needed a modicum of normalcy and would never have it living as we were. So I explained to Mother that I was going to get an apartment not far from her—that I would be nearby if she needed me. (Thank the Lord, she was in decent health throughout all of this.) I said that Ramona and the baby would live with me until they got on their feet. She accepted the idea almost before I could get the words out of my mouth, and I wonder to this day what took me so long to figure out the solution.

Myra speaks well of her mother and does not blame her for the fact that she and her granddaughter could not get along. Myra chalks it up to generational differences. "Everyone's relationship improved from day one when we moved into our own place."

Some months later Myra commented on how things are going today.

Mother still gets jealous when I'm involved after work or on weekends with Ramona and the baby—going places or just playing in the apartment. Although my daughter shares an apartment with her live-in boyfriend, she still likes to come by some evenings or on a weekend and just hang out with Mom/Grandma—meaning me. But then my mother calls, and you can hear the strain in her voice. She is feeling left out. So now I try to have Sunday dinners at my place and invite them all. I want to be inclusive and be the catalyst for this family, but at times, I must admit that I get tired after working all week and doing so much "go-betweening." It's exhausting to be all things to all people! But I suspect when Ramona marries (which appears to be soon), I will have more time for Mother. I can do less grandparenting, as Emily will have a dad!

When asked why Emily and Ramona had moved out of her apartment, Myra explained: "She needed her 'own domain' [as grandmother Pat so aptly phrased it]—to be with people her own age. When you have reached womanhood, you need to be on your own. I could readily identify with my daughter's desire for a measure of independence. I was in her shoes once. And although I had become very attached to the baby, I did nothing to stop my daughter from going off on her own."

Myra's four-generational family is not unlike many in this new era of greater longevity. As the Census Bureau noted in a November 1992 report, more and more American families will be made up of four generations instead of two or three, as a result of a phenomenal growth in the nation's elderly population.

This new wave of multigenerational families has mixed implications. On the one hand, more children will grow up with the emotional, physical, and financial support of grandparents and great-grandparents (and assorted older relatives). But on the other hand, more people in their sixties (sometimes referred to as the "sandwiched generation") will be called upon to care for the eighty- and ninety-year-olds.

Couple this emotional, physical, and financial drain with assisting divided families—note the divorce rate hovering at 49 percent and the significant rise in single-parent homes, especially those headed by women (who historically have a lower standard of living than men)—and you have the dilemma of the "sandwiched generation."

Elaine Brody, a researcher and author who popularized the term "women in the middle," describes the increasingly common burdens faced by middle-aged women. She states that many are now taking care of elderly parents while trying to manage households, maintain careers, and help children who may still live at home or who have returned to the "nest" because of divorce and/or economic problems.

Researchers are seeing whole groups of women quitting their jobs because they simply cannot juggle the day-to-day care of an elderly parent along with the added responsibilities of returning children and grandchildren.

There are hopeful signs, however, that growing numbers of businesses, as well as government agencies, are becoming more sensitized to the burdens borne by "those in the middle." Some companies are going out of their way to proclaim themselves "family friendly." In 1992, nearly one hundred and forty of them set up a nationwide program to upgrade child-care programs or set up on-site day care for their workers. In a similar move, NationsBank Corporation announced it would spend thirty-five million dollars to subsidize its workers' child care and to build or upgrade dependent-care facilities.

Other employers offer chits or vouchers to employees seeking day care for aging and/or sickly parents or for the overwhelming part of our workforce who still have children at home. More and more corporations are finding that the answer to getting their employees to give more is to make it easier for workers to balance work and family. Studies indicate a higher degree of productivity when workers are not stressed and torn between job and home.

MARTHA'S STORY: DEVISING A PLAN AND GETTING EVERYONE BEHIND IT

Martha and her husband, Edward, are active, healthy grandparents in their early sixties. When I interviewed Martha, her father was cognitively impaired as a result of suffering a series of small strokes. He required a support system to keep him going in his own apartment (i.e., assistance in food preparation, bathing, and getting to and from places). Martha's dad was about eighty when Martha and Edward's daughter and two grandchildren came home to live with them temporarily.

"Talk about being stressed out!" confides Martha. She discusses these stresses and how she went about easing them:

Eddie was working his old-style ten-hour days. He couldn't even contemplate retirement. Our daughter had received a paltry sum of child support, and she couldn't find a job for close to a year! Dad only had his social security check to live on, and it just didn't cover all his expenses.

My grandchildren were especially in want of a stable, continuous reaching out of nurturance. Our daughter was shaky emotionally for quite a while, too.

The first thing I did was to put most of my volunteer obligations on hold, at least temporarily. They were pulling me in too many directions.

I initially sought assistance from a local family service agency in how to deal effectively with my father so that I would not be consumed with his caretaking needs. I had to consider blocks of time and how to use my time wisely and where best to place my efforts. I soon realized that there wasn't enough of Martha to go around! Also, three warm bodies had just moved in with us after we had been alone for twelve years!

Martha offers sage advice to other grandparents and parents as she balances the needs of her daughter, grandchildren, and father: "I think it helps to know you can persevere. You need an agenda, a plan, a few allies on your side. Until there is agreement by all parties concerned," declares Martha, "it won't fly!"

Martha shares something she learned over the years: "A woman needs to constantly reinvent herself with each stage of life." She adds, "You have to move above self-pity. And the doubts and resistance of your old-fashioned husband. Even if he doesn't 'cotton' to counseling, do your best to get him (and the whole family) into a few sessions. It's a nonadversarial approach to understanding and solving problems before family relationships deteriorate sometimes beyond repair. And write a contract (I do mean 'written'), which spells out who is going to do what!"

Martha's theory is that a grandparent can exert a potent effect on the lives of grandchildren who are wandering through the no-man's-land of their parents' separation and ultimate divorce. This is borne out by many findings of experts. But this positive effect can be diluted if there is a lot of bickering and nitpicking about who is supposed to do what. Who is to take Billy to the dentist, or pick up Betsy's school supplies, or fix the lunches for school, or do the kids' laundry, or cook the dinner, or clean up the toys before bedtime, or empty the ever-full dishwasher?

And if a newly labeled single daughter or son, now living at home, is not adhering to house rules, then these rules may need to be clarified further or perhaps modified in some way or to be mediated or reworked so as to be more feasible and clearly defined.

Mental health experts recommend that, when possible, day-to-day care of children should be in the hands of the custodial parent, with a grandparent as a support person or in an auxiliary or substitute role. Grandparents and parents should have ongoing discussions about discipline, bedtime, and bathing rituals, cleanliness habits, food rules, and so on. All such matters should be agreed on in advance or as the process moves along. As grandmother Martha notes, "Take nothing for granted, and don't assume anything!"

Martha explained that through a family service association she found someone who assisted her with maintaining her father in his apartment. She paid this individual an hourly wage that was based on her father's Social Security benefits. The caregiver visited her dad for three hours in the morning and three hours in the late afternoon to help with his bathing, dressing, and meal preparation. Other services performed included dispensing medication, driving her father to the doctor, doing his laundry, and straightening up the apartment. This took a load off Martha. Then she arranged with the nearby senior citizens center to have its van transport her dad to and from the center each day. There he was served a hot meal at noon and could socialize with his peers. On weekends, Martha had her dad over for Sunday dinner at her house, where he would mingle with his great-grandchildren, granddaughter, daughter, and son-in-law.

When her daughter went back to work, here is what Martha did about child care: "We found a combination nursery school and day care for our three-year-old granddaughter so she was taken care of until four o'clock each weekday. Our grandson went to the nearby public school. I kept the children at my house from four until five-thirty, two or three days a week. Our daughter arranged for a sitter the other days. It all worked out—but it definitely did require lots of planning and organization."

FLORENCE AND JAMES'S STORY:
INVOLVING THE WHOLE FAMILY

"Because of our grandson's teenage aunts and uncles, two of whom were still living at home with us, I think Little Jim was strengthened during and after the divorce," observes grandfather James. "When he and his mother moved in with us, he was everybody's 'Little Jim Boy'!"

Still, there's a price to pay. Florence reminds her husband that although this fact may have been to the good of Little Jim, there was a loss of privacy, not only for them but for their teenage children as well. As Florence reports, "Although our other kids loved the baby and were a vital part of his first years, our other children were deprived of a certain amount of interaction with us as parents. By necessity, there is a natural disruption when a mother and child move home. And a small child usually wins hands down in drawing the attention of adults!"

According to Florence, "The youngest of our clan was the most affected because she had little or no time with Mom." And it was the friction between the oldest (the daughter who had moved home) and her youngest daughter that was the most difficult part of the moving in. "I was always the 'middleman,'" Florence laments, "trying to get things to run smoothly—soothing ruffled feathers."

Dr. Karen Lewis, an expert in the field of sibling relations, thinks that the grandmother in this situation needed to talk things out with each of her daughters separately and then with both of them together. Dr. Lewis believes that the younger daughter probably felt displaced—left out—and that if Florence could have gotten her daughter involved with some of Little Jim's child care, she would perhaps have felt more a part of everything. It also would have been helpful if Florence did something with her youngest daughter on a weekly basis, just mother and daughter, a special something that the younger daughter enjoys doing with Mom.

Florence responded to a question about how much her husband

had helped out. "Well, you know men, they do what they want when they choose to." She and James play traditional roles.

James and his wife, Florence, believe that it's necessary to have a positive outlook—"It's one hundred percent attitude"—and that maintaining a good working relationship with Little Jim's father, who lived not too far away, was instrumental in the boy's adjustment. "I think the hard work we carried on to show Little Jim that we cared about his father and that our door was open to his dad was to Little Jim's advantage," says James. Florence adds that they stressed the importance of all being considerate of one another.

The family did not seek any type of family therapy for the conflict between the siblings. James notes that they are a very private family—used to working things out on their own.

This statement is in keeping with the thinking that is typical of this generation of grandparents. Marc Rabinowitz says, "Only recently did people begin to think of, or talk about, or question what was out of their control. It is this generation's mode of thinking that they simply do what is required of them. They don't question responsibility and they are not open to complaining about personal matters."

One wonders whether this is so because of purely generational differences or partly because of ethnic traditions or the pioneer/frontier mentality.

As we saw in the preceding chapter, many adults in the age range between fifty and seventy (and beyond) are still uncomfortable in seeking outside help. These "nonbelievers" feel that any type of therapy, counseling, or even joining a support group casts aspersions on their parenting skills. Some are convinced that something is deficient in their character if they are unable to cope with a chaotic or difficult situation.

When Florence found that scarcely anything she said or did helped to solve much of the friction between her daughters, she decided as a matter of survival to go back to work part-time, because, as she put it, "If I wasn't there, things somehow got done and the majority of the differences were usually resolved by the time I got home."

When probed about the effect on her marriage by this moving in of a young parent with a child, Florence asserted that they had been used to a lack of privacy anyway, having a house full of children and teens. James gave a little wink when asked about the subject of intimacy, or lack of same.

"Our best friends loaned us their beach cottage and every three or four weeks, we'd just take off, the two of us, for a long weekend," was Jim's retort. Florence was caught off guard for a moment, as James usually keeps such things very close to the vest. She blushed a bit.

JANICE AND HERB'S STORY: TOO MUCH INVOLVEMENT?

"Although I dreamed of having my grandchildren living in the same city where Herb and I lived," bemoans Janice, "their coming home to live with us for almost eight months was one of the most difficult times in our life. There is this great pull or desire to help, but you are torn about how much—and your life is turned inside out."

Janice explains why her daughter, Valerie, decided to come home:

When my daughter called from her home in Connecticut to say she and our two grandchildren just couldn't hack it without some type of a family support system or safety net, I wasn't really surprised. They had tried by themselves for almost a year, and we knew, Herb and I, that our daughter was not emotionally grounded enough (due to the traumatic divorce and all) to handle those kids by herself. Our former son-in-law was not actively involved with the children, nor were his parents who lived right there. Thank goodness, Valerie had *wonderful friends there for her, but as she soon realized, friends are not family. They all had their own families and their own problems to attend to.*

"We were their lifeboat, and I liken the operation to a rescue at sea," says Herb. He continues the story:

It always seemed pointless to me to wonder whether or not we actually wanted to do this. Look, they needed a hell of a lot more than good ol' Dad putting them up in some apartment! What they needed and got was Jan and me—and some good old-fashioned hands-on parenting and grandparenting. Those kids had been through hell and back. Their lives had been torn apart when their dad left. And our daughter, well, she needed everything: encouragement, love, affection, empathy, and, as a single mom, help in raising those kids. And then there was the money. My ex-son-in-law was always late with the little bit of money he could afford to pay for child support. He had gone bankrupt and made next to nothing in his new job.

Our youngest grandson used to say, "If it wasn't for Grandpa, we'd be homeless!" It's aggravating when you get to this stage in life where we are. I kid about it on one hand, but it's frightening. I'm at the age where a lot of my friends are retiring, and I'm spending chunks of money on lawyers, mental health specialists, shelter, and food for my daughter and grandchildren. But what were we to do, let them go on welfare?

Val is terrific with the kids! We were always close to them—used to go up there a lot and visit. So we were, like they say, "bonded" at the outset, even before they got here. Of course, I was working every day, so a lot of the credit goes to Jan. Problem was she, Jan that is, is a natural-born caretaker, and I had to slow her down a bit, before she was doing everything. I tried talking with Valerie about this and had to straighten her out a few times about her letting Mom do most of the child care and chores around the place. Finally, I had to put my foot down—draw the parameters so to speak. Jan was in her early sixties and although full of energy and in good health, her stamina just wasn't what it was when she was raising our three children thirty years ago! . . . But eventually, after a lot of family meetings around the dining room table (and talking it out) like we did when our own kids were young, we parceled off the housekeeping, set up a schedule for who cooked dinner on what nights, et cetera. Baby-sitting by Jan and me was set up on a limited basis, and the decisions were laid out as to additional laundry and cleaning and who picked up the kids after school and just who was responsible for what. (Actually, we wrote them on a piece of cardboard—a regular chart.) I'm an old Navy C.O., and I know that for a ship to run smoothly you have to have a system and delegate the work.

Looking back on the experience, Janice says: "Although I believe that we helped restore a sense of balance and a degree of normalcy to Val and the children, it was a terrible drain on our resources. Maybe we went overboard and should have done less. I don't know. Guess it's not our style to do things halfheartedly!"

Janice and Herb's story illustrates that even if you do go overboard in a crisis situation, it's possible to negotiate the terms of the living arrangements when things settle down. Ideally, of course, it's best to come to an agreement in advance. And remember that this agreement can be renegotiated later if necessary. (Refer back to chapter 4 for a discussion on the importance of setting limits.)

Valerie and her two children have their own place now, in the same city where Herb and Janice live, and life is getting back to normal—almost.

When asked about the present, Janice gives a generally positive response, although there is some uneasiness about the degree of involvement she and Herb still have.

Val still calls me a lot to help out. Sometimes I feel up to it. Other times I wish it was of my own choosing. Yet I do understand and empathize about the stress of being a single parent, especially a work-

ing single parent and having to raise your children by yourself. TV
and movies make it look glamorous. Believe me, I'm glad I didn't
have to go to work and leave my children when they were young. So
I help out during the week when I can. We found it easier to have a
set schedule. But I'm learning to be more flexible in case one of the
children is sick and Valerie can't take off from work. I share certain
days with a baby-sitter, and we keep the children until Val picks
them up after school. It's only a couple of afternoons a week, so it's
fine. I don't like the idea of my grandchildren being with a sitter five
days a week—and besides, my daughter doesn't make enough to
cover all her baby-sitting expenses. I think the children like coming
here—and we have fun.

Because there is no active daddy, Herb and I try to do something
with the kids for a few hours either Saturday or Sunday. This also
gives Val a few hours to herself. And about once a month the children spend the night. So all in all, we have a pretty good system of
what we consider a reasonable involvement and keeping a strong
grandparental enrichment going. Yet we still have time for ourselves
and each other. Oh, naturally, from time to time, there are conflicts,
but we talk them out. It's a balancing act, all right, which we are
still perfecting!

Jan reflects on a recent evening. "Soon after Val and the kids
moved out, Herb came in and I didn't have the TV news hour on
or the radio or stereo. I was just sitting in my favorite chair reading
a book and relishing the sounds of my home—even the humming
of our appliances. Herb walked over and gave me a big hug,
propped up his feet on his ottoman, and we both said out loud, at
the same moment, 'We're all alone!' "

KAY AND MARVIN'S STORY: TAKING IN A SINGLE DAD AND HIS SONS

When Kay and Marvin speak about the impact of their son's divorce, it's apparent that although it was a veritable struggle at

times, they managed to serve as surrogate parents to two small boys, who, like leaves that had been whipped up in a windstorm, found a new peace in its aftermath.

Our son Ted and our grandsons, Timmy and Eric, tried to live on their own up in Michigan after Catherine walked out. We thought a lot about Ted and his loneliness for Catherine. We could feel for him . . . he had no one beside him who was aware of his comings and goings and to share his disappointments and his accomplishments. We hated to think of that grown kid of ours all alone. Of course, he had the boys—but they were so young, he couldn't emote or share his feelings with them. We managed to get together either here or there as often as we could!

She and Ted never got along. I don't know why they bothered to have children. But we adore those grandsons, so I'm glad they had them. Catherine asked for no financial support, just to be able to see the boys three or four times a year. When the boys are older, I don't think they'll have a thing to do with her. But we learned not to knock their mother; they'll make their own judgments. And we have always pleaded with Ted not to say anything negative about the boys' mother, at least not in front of them. And he is catching on. He sees that it only makes the boys more insecure.

Well, after about a year or so of trying to work and be both mother and father to the boys, Ted realized the children needed more of a support system—more family.

Marvin and I had been alone for quite some time and had gotten kind of used to the privacy—all that peace and quiet. (Sometimes, it was too quiet, maybe even a little boring!) So when Ted approached us about coming home to live with the boys, just till they got on their feet, we knew this would be best for all three of them [and] we said yes immediately. (I think Catherine must have known we would help Ted raise those youngsters!)

I couldn't believe what had happened to our upbeat, cheerful son. He came home like a sleepwalker or a zombie! He was still in a state of shock, I think, about the way Catherine had just left. And the little guys? Well, they cried a lot, fought more than I ever remember, woke up at night with bad dreams, and the littlest one started wetting his bed again. They had regressed, to be sure. Ted had always been an involved dad, but he seemed unable to parent. His life was on hold. And he needed as much TLC as the boys did!

So here we were, in our sixties, active in our church, traveling a lot now that Marvin had retired. And here come two little boys who needed raising. All I can say is: Our life wasn't boring any longer or quiet!

After a few months, Ted seemed to regain some of his old vigor and started parenting again and playing with the boys more. He started keeping himself up and talked about looking for a job. He even mentioned dating again, so we knew he was on the mend. After three or four months, Ted found work. We put Timmy and Eric in our church day care, just blocks from our home. Ted dropped them off in the morning, and Marvin or I would get them in the afternoon.

I don't have to tell you what an adjustment this was for both Marvin and me! But I think it worked out all right. Marvin was a great help, with the extra grocery shopping and playing with the boys. If he hadn't been retired, I sometimes wonder what I would have done. Marvin was a good disciplinarian, too, in a firm, loving way. They knew who was in charge!

Marvin and I had been used to a lot of privacy. This was really our main complaint. But as senior citizens, we are entitled to discounts at certain motels or hotels—and so about once a month, we'd take off when Ted came home on a Friday after the work week, and he could take care of the boys. We'd go away, not doing much or spending a lot of money—just having some quiet time and being by ourselves.

After about a year, Ted came to us and told us he had a girlfriend and was going to move in with her. We were a little upset about this and voiced our opinion about how this relationship would affect the boys, who were then three and six. The boys had just gotten used to being with us, and we didn't think they should move again, and how was this "live-in" thing going to play out? Ted assured us it wasn't just a fling; they were going to be married soon. But Ted ran up against a stone wall with the boys. We stayed out of it, but they would not leave "Gammy" and "Gampy." They were attached to us, all right. So Ted moved in with his girlfriend anyway, and the boys stayed with us. Eventually, the boys did go to live with their dad. Ted married Jeanne, and she is good to the boys. Funny thing, though, Timmy and Eric still treat us more like parents than grandparents!

Ted and his new wife, Jeanne, work long hours, so we keep the boys after school. But it's all right. We feel we have the best of both worlds. We see the kids for about an hour or two each day, and when they leave to go home, we have our private time back.

I believe things have a way of working out, if you have the proper attitude and don't dramatize everything out of proportion. Marvin and I knew we were in this for the long haul. We have a good relationship with our son Ted and our new daughter-in-law. We make very few demands. And don't give advice unless it's asked, and then, only sparingly. Our grandsons are extremely close to us.

Ted's brothers live near here, and when Timmy and Eric moved in with us it brought this family together. Having loving aunts, uncles, and cousins around has given the boys stability and a sense of family.

SALLY'S STORY: A WIDOW'S GAINS AND LOSSES

Sally had been a widow for only five months when her daughter and grandson came to live with her.

He saved my life! If it weren't for my grandson, Josh, who was about three years old when he and my daughter moved in with me,

I would have kept on wallowing in self-pity over the death of my husband.

I was letting myself go and was apathetic about everything. But I couldn't let Josh see me like that so I pulled myself together. He needed me! Through his eyes and ears, I started to see the wonders of nature once again. I had always loved the beach, but because I was reminded of the strolls and good times Bill and I used to have there, I stopped going. But when I began to take care of Josh, on the days his mother did her nursing, I began to revel in his excitement or exploring. It was like I had awoke from a deep sleep!

BARBARA AND FRED'S STORY: RECONCILING GENERATIONAL DIFFERENCES

When Barbara and Fred's daughter, Jamie, and two young grandchildren moved in with them, their traditional marriage was disrupted, and Barbara and Jamie clashed over their different parenting styles.

Barbara gives some background information:

We have a long-term marriage. Unusual in this day and age. But it has not been accomplished without a lot of work and listening to each other's problems and having time for the general attentiveness women of my generation are accustomed to giving their men. Although I worked out of the home periodically after the children were grown, I had to face the fact that mine was an old-fashioned marriage. We always did better when we were alone—before the children came along and after they left the nest.

My husband's work has built-in pressure. So you can picture him coming home at seven in the evening to two little people jumping all over him, clamoring for his attention—rambunctious tots that Fred dearly loves, of course. But all he wanted to do was to sit down with cocktail in hand, listen to the MacNeil-Lehrer news hour, have a quiet dinner with me, with each of us making inquiries as to the day's events. Then his usual ritual would be to read the paper, uninterrupted, and perhaps watch a show or two on TV with only an occasional incoming phone call to mar the peaceful solitude.

Barbara says that their daughter had a horrendous divorce; very wrenching, as she termed it. And as she recalls:

We welcomed her home with the children. They had no other place to go. They needed a loving, warm family around. And they did flourish within the bosom of this nurturing grandmother (and grandfather!). We felt for all of them, but to be perfectly honest, I wasn't sure at times that we would survive. Two women in the same kitchen? Young children, seemingly everywhere, with toys, Popsicles, crumbs, crayons? And then there was the requisite amount of crying and vying for attention. Oh, and don't forget the extra laundry, cooking, shopping, and cleaning up.

Philosophically, my daughter and I had tremendous differences as to parenting. I had never been a permissive parent. And she is just that. Oh, she's a loving, caring mother, mind you, but I think that working mothers have a tendency to give in too much; indulge, perhaps to make up for their absence. Whatever the reasons, we had a lot of mediating, and talking it out in order to find a reasonable dialogue (and respect) necessary to living in the same house.

Dr. Karen Lewis strongly urges grandparents to keep reminding themselves that the children belong to the mother. "Put your advice list in the medicine cabinet. Take it out once in a while and look at it. But don't show it to your daughter or son, and don't discuss it. Since even before *Hamlet*, parents have been telling their grown children how to parent. Look what they're doing (or mostly not doing) with *their* children!"

And as Dr. Lewis notes, unless there are serious concerns such as possible neglect or abuse, it's best to keep in mind the impor-

tance of assisting one's child in regaining his or her parental autonomy. Dr. Lewis further comments that this approach will be the
impetus for an improved relationship between parent and adult son
or daughter.

Dr. Lewis does not recommend interceding by a father on behalf of either mother or daughter, or both. She subscribes to the
theory that "they have to work it out by themselves as two adults."
She suggests that "when the father tries to play referee, it demeans
the relationship between the mother and daughter. It's as if they
were still two children. Grandmother should have a sense of confidence in what she says and does and project that confidence in a
'talk-it-out-with-*me*' attitude."

Dr. Lewis further discusses this generation of grandmothers'
concerns that to be assertive risks being labeled a "deficient" grandmother. "Grandmothers should not be afraid to protect their own
interests," says Dr. Lewis, "as well as those of the grandchildren
and the moving-in child. They really need to ask themselves,
'What about me?' Grandmothers are often women who have been
used to doing for others—the 'enablers.' They actually forget to
look out for themselves. Repeatedly the question must be raised, 'Is
this in my best interest, too?' "

A grandmother should not assume that her husband understands her situation fully or that he will automatically come to her
aid. Dr. Lewis: "He may not notice things about you and your live-
at-home child and grandchildren, just as he didn't take note of you
and your children in these situations. He may see that you are being
used too much in his intellectual sort of way, yet he doesn't really
see it. Therefore, you have to let him know what you assume he
does know, but he doesn't; and that is: he has to give to you more."

Dr. Lewis also remarks that "women are more in tune or more
aware of the fact that they need privacy and as a couple, time together. You may have to talk about it openly, and sensitize and
heighten your husband's awareness. This is the basic intuitiveness
of women versus men."

Fred and Barbara were used to making love in the morning, especially in the years since their youngest had left for college. "But forget it," Fred recalls, "Barbara wasn't comfortable with Jamie and the kids in the house. Besides, she was exhausted most of the time." After three months of abstinence, Barbara suggested to Fred that they go away for a weekend, and he halfheartedly agreed. "We did go once or twice, but I was too drained to think about it or plan it. I wanted Fred to arrange it. He seemed too depressed to take the initiative."

Depression is all too common in men of Fred's age. Dr. Lewis explains: "Many men are already in the transition stage of their life at this point. They were probably feeling depressed even before the arrival of the grandchildren and adult child. They are starting to wind down their career; they are feeling less competent. Men take their rewards and gratification from their work, not from their home life, which is basically the old issue of the devaluation of women's work. If men can transfer or rework their gratification to other parts of their life, such as family, the transition will be helped and there will be less depression."

Barbara, for her part, relied on exercise to lift her spirits. But her exercise routine was interrupted when her daughter and grand-children moved in. Says Barbara: "I couldn't figure out how to find time for . . . exercise. Finally, I explained to my daughter, Jamie, that just as she had done when she lived in her own home, she could take care of the girls without my help in the early morning hours. (I liked the early morning to run or fast walk.)"

As time went on, Barbara learned to set limits in other areas as well. As she explains: "It became apparent each day that more and more of my caretaking ways were being exploited. When I was asked to baby-sit more than I felt comfortable with, I explained lovingly, but firmly, that at our age and stage in life, we needed time alone and time together, and that I or Dad or we were available one evening a week, period!"

Dr. Lewis praises Barbara for setting limits in a cordial, nonangry way. She also advises grandmothers to be very up front with the daughter or son. Make clear statements, and never assume anything!

Although they did their best to cope with the situation, Barbara and Fred eventually sought family counseling to alleviate some of the stress. They brought along their daughter, Jamie, and the children as well. "Jamie came around to the realization we weren't a couple of kids any longer," declares Fred, "and that the only way it would work was if she pitched in more and did the bulk of the mothering and help with the household chores. We were also guided by the professionals to see that a more scientific approach, with a contract designating who was responsible for what, was a necessary implement in this family structure."

No longer finding it necessary to be Supergrandma, Barbara could realistically face her challenges. "I shouldn't have waited to feel as if I was being swallowed up or under siege," Barbara concludes, "because by the time you feel that way, it's late, and a lot of the damage is done to you personally and to your close relationships."

As one professional expressed it, "If we have a terrible physical ache or pain, we attend to it. We see a doctor in a matter of days or weeks, not months. Why, then, do we procrastinate when emotional needs are present and we find ourselves in chaos or not coping well?"

From the range of degrees of involvement exhibited by the grandparents profiled in this chapter, I suspect that just as each of us has an individual threshold for withstanding physical pain, so it is with assessing at what point "a little" becomes "too much" interaction.

But whatever the amount of involvement, the desire to lend support, safeguard, and empower a family in difficulty is at the core of every case history in this chapter. These grandparents are providing sanctuaries, offering safe passage to loved ones battered by the raging storm of divorce.

6.
The Legal Rights
of Grandparents

§

VISITATION

AND

CUSTODY

As the parent of a divorced child, you may find yourself in a situation where you must take legal action to see your grandchildren on a regular basis. In more extreme circumstances, you may even end up petitioning the court for custody of these grandchildren. What are the legal rights of grandparents in this regard? In the following discussion, we will examine the issues of visitation and custody—from the gains that grandparents have made to the work that still needs to be done.

VISITATION

The right to petition a court in order to see your grandchild was not a guaranteed right in this country before 1975 in a majority of states.

In the last two decades or so, state legislatures have given an edge to grandparents as they seek court-ordered visitation with their grandchildren. Presently, every state has a statute that enables grandparents (and in some states—siblings, relatives, or other persons) to petition for visitation rights. (See appendix B for a state-by-state listing.)

Until these statutes were enacted, grandparents could obtain visitation only if they demonstrated that a child could be harmed if visitation rights were *not* granted. Now, grandparents can obtain court-ordered visitation if they can persuade a court that visitation would be better for the child—a much easier task.

The overturning of long-standing legal precedent has been due in large part to the proliferation and greater visibility of grandparents' rights organizations, which have heightened the awareness of state legislatures, jurists, and the legal profession as a whole. These organizations and social scientists have attuned us to the critical importance of the grandparent-grandchild relationship. The courts have mirrored this philosophy in recognizing the indispensable nature of this attachment.

Dr. Arthur Kornhaber, a founder of the grandparent movement, asserts, "It has only been in the last twenty years that U.S. jurisprudence has begrudgingly begun to recognize the importance of grandparents to grandchildren and to support this view of the family structure through law."

History tells us that courts often lag behind as reluctant players while society forges ahead within the bounds of new mores. The dilemmas that naturally flow from change become society's charge long before the courts wrestle with its resulting ambiguities.

Reminding us that there are no absolutes in grandparent visitation, Dr. Kornhaber suggests that "a day in court does not automatically win the case." As he observes, "When a child is adopted by strangers or a child's custodian remarries, natural grandparents can possibly be pushed out of the family portrait."

Many legal experts admonish grandparents to obtain legal representation by a family law specialist in such cases. If funds are not available for hiring an attorney, it is still possible to fight for and win visitation by working independently. (Some of the legal practitioners you will meet later in this chapter suggest how this can be accomplished as a "Do-it-yourselfer.")

What brought about the phenomenal growth of the grandparents' rights movement? With a burgeoning divorce rate, resulting in tumultuous family breakups and divided families, grandparents quite naturally have felt they could help fill the void created in the family.

Grandparents' rights organizations have increased in number as more and more grandparents have felt estranged from their grandchildren. Sometimes this estrangement comes about because of remarriage by one or both parents or a strained relationship with the custodial parent or simply out of vengeance by one of the parents. As alienation grows within the divided family, many grandparents find themselves awash in controversy. The link to their grandchildren is disconnected or weakened.

Because of the naturalness of the grandparent bond, these alienated grandparents have formed alliances, knowing full well of the strength that comes from numbers and solidarity of purpose. These grandparents have vocalized their powerful sentiments along with the statistics. They have produced a marked shift in social policy on grandparents' rights.

Grandparents' gains are not unlimited. Again, no statute gives grandparents an absolute right to visitation with grandchildren. Instead, these relatively new laws give grandparents the *right to petition* for visitation. As noted earlier, courts grant visitation *only* if it is determined that such visitation is in the best interest of the child.

While most grandparent visitation cases are settled by the ruling statute of a particular state, it is nevertheless important for you to recognize the inherent powers of juvenile and family court judges. Their primary goal is to protect the child's best interest under the courts' doctrine of *parens patriae*. (*Parens patriae* is the state's sovereignty or power of guardianship over minors.) In some cases, the court *may* be able to award grandparental visitation *even* in the absence of explicit statutory authority.

A bit of historical perspective: Beginning in the 1800s and well into the 1970s, courts, in denying petitions for extending grandparental visitation, alluded to the notion of a compelling parental right. The courts believed that parents had complete control over the upbringing of any child in their custody. It was cited in these early cases that grandparent visitation acted as a constraint upon that control and therefore was not in the child's best interest. Exceptions to this way of thinking were few. They occurred in situations where the parent was deemed unfit, or the child had lived with the grandparent, or the parties to a divorce proceeding agreed to the visitation, or the visitation was intended to preserve family ties after one parent had died.

Under common-law principles, grandparents did not have *any* legal right to visit and to communicate with their grandchild if such visitation or communication was forbidden by the parents.

The reasoning behind this rule of law was that any judicial enforcement of grandparent visitation rights would divide and hinder parental authority. Thus, the courts argued, the best interest of a minor child would not be furthered by forcing a child into the midst of a conflict of authority and ill feeling between parent and grandparent. One might conclude that the courts viewed the parent's obligation to allow grandparental visitation as a moral one rather than a legal one.

Now, however, two U.S. Supreme Court decisions have upheld the rights of grandparents to visit grandchildren in families where parents object. The court left intact an existing law in Wisconsin. Two weeks earlier, the high court let stand a similar law in Kentucky. Here are brief summaries of these two cases:

King v. *King*, 828 S.W.2d 630 (Ky 1992): Stewart and Anne King are under court order to allow W. R. King, paternal grandfather of their five-year-old daughter, Jessica, visitation twice a week.

The U.S. Supreme Court denied review of a Kentucky Circuit

Court decision, permitting the grandfather visitation for a two-hour period each Wednesday and Saturday. The justices, without comment, refused to rule that the law unconstitutionally interferes with the parents' right to raise their children as they wish, or interferes with the parents' Fourteenth Amendment liberty interest, or is not in the child's best interests.

The Kings once lived in a house that W. R. King, Jessica's grandfather, had built for them on his farm in Boyle County. Stewart King, who worked at a factory in Danville, worked on the farm in return for living rent free and a portion of the proceeds from the farm's tobacco crop. A rift developed between the two King men, and Stewart King's family moved away from the farm in 1988. W. R. King, the father of Stewart King, asked if he could visit Jessica on occasion. When her parents refused, he sued. A state judge awarded Mr. King, Sr., permanent visitation rights, ordering the Kings to let Jessica see her grandfather for a few hours each Wednesday and Saturday. The judge relied on a state law allowing for such visitation rights if found to be in the child's best interests.

A state appeals court reversed the judge's ruling after deciding Jessica's best interests had not been addressed, but the Kentucky Supreme Court reinstated the visitation order in March 1992 and the U.S. Supreme Court has now upheld that decision by the Kentucky Supreme Court, reinstating the grandfather's visitation rights.

The Kentucky high court observed that:

The grandparents' visitation statute was an appropriate response to the change in the demographics of domestic relations, mirrored by the dramatic increase in the divorce rate and in the number of children born to unmarried parents, and the increasing independence and alienation within the extended family inherent in a mobile society. There is no reason that a petty dispute between a father and son should be allowed to deprive a grandparent and grandchild of the unique relationship that ordinarily exists between those individuals.

One of the main purposes of the statute is to prevent a family quarrel of little significance to disrupt a relationship which should be encouraged rather than destroyed.

In the second case, the Court of Appeals of Wisconsin wrote in an opinion that adoption severs all rights of the adopted child's birth family. And as a result, this would terminate the grandparents' status as grandparents. (From *Official Wisconsin Reports: In the Matter of C.G.F. 168 Wis. 2d 62.*)

The Supreme Court of Wisconsin, however, concluded that the Court of Appeals incorrectly ruled, and reversed the opinion. (Reversing 163 Wis. 2d 1094, 474 N.W.2d 530 [Ct.App.1991].) Since Wisconsin law defines a parent as either a biological parent or a parent by adoption, the deceased parent in this case continues to be considered the parent and therefore the deceased *parent's parents* should continue to be considered grandparents. The Supreme Court of Wisconsin added the following:

Once the grandparents in this case were ordered visitation rights with their minor grandchild, they should not have been deprived of those rights without due process. Because Section 880.155, Stats., allows grandparent visitation to continue subsequent to adoption of the child, we reverse the decision of the Court of Appeals. . . .

A trial court's authority to grant grandparent visitation pursuant to Section 880.155, Stats., continues even after subsequent adoption. The statute allows the trial court, in the best interest of the child, to order grandparental visitation in direct opposition to the wishes of the custodian regardless of who the custodian is.

(For further information on adoption and visitation, see the discussion at the end of this section.)

Thus, the issue of whether grandparent visitation orders unconstitutionally infringe upon the right of parents to parent has at long last been addressed by the highest courts of this nation. Petitions of visitation awarded to grandparents over the protestations and express wishes of parents or stepparents are occurring more frequently and are being reviewed more favorably by our courts in all fifty states. The mere fact that a parent(s) does not desire grandparental visitation cannot *by itself* be sufficient reason for denying that visitation. Antagonism between the grandparent and the custodian parent, resulting from monetary disputes, for example, are insufficient reason to cut off the visitation. But note that court-ordered visitation by grandparents is favored by the courts *only* on condition that the grandparent-grandchild relationship is one of stability and proper influence.

These new statutes create a presumption that the best interests of the child are ordinarily served by maintaining contact with grandparents unless otherwise proven.

The following words are reflections by a jurist from the New Jersey Supreme Court: "It is a biological fact that grandparents are bound to their grandchildren by the unbreakable link of heredity. Visits with a grandparent are often a precious part of a child's experience, and there are benefits which devolve upon the grandchild which he cannot derive from any other relationship. Neither the legislature nor this court is blind to human truths which grandparents and grandchildren have always known."

Why has the pendulum swung toward grandparents' rights? Given the consistently high divorce rate in this country, the state has a compelling interest in protecting a child's emotional health through visitation with an important third party, usually a grandparent. There are other reasons for changes in the law, as well. Take the graying of America. The courts have construed that "new-age" grandparents are not so aged any longer. Today's grandparents are a vital force in our populace.

Approximately 75 percent of all older Americans are grandparents. An estimated one million of their grandchildren each year will experience the divorce of their parents. In addition, older

Americans have become more outspoken in expressing their concerns. There is a general willingness now to litigate family matters.

While all fifty states statutorily provide an avenue by which grandparents can petition the courts for visitation with their grandchildren over a parent's wishes, let us examine another subtlety in all of this "court watching." Originally, this type of legislation was intended to allow grandparents to maintain an *existing* relationship with a grandchild following the dissolution of the parents' marriage. Now, however, grandparent visitation laws have been expanded to include an *opportunity to begin* a relationship with a grandchild, or to visit with a grandchild following the child's adoption by a stepparent, or to visit with a grandchild who has been surrendered to an agency for adoption.

Founder and director of the Grandparents Rights Organization, Attorney Richard S. Victor of Michigan, claims that "grandparents' rights to visitation are only one half of the coin." The other half, says Victor, deals with the rights of grandchildren who have been denied the ability to communicate with and maintain contact with their grandparents. "Children denied the right to share experiences and memories with their grandparents as they grow are denied the security of 'unconditional' love that grandparents offer to grandchildren."

Victor backs up his views with research that has demonstrated a child's need for stability and continuity of meaningful relationships. "The recognition of visitation rights should be entrusted to the sound discretion of courts. But if the best interests of children is a meaningful legal concept, it is clear that it is sound policy to nurture, rather than sever, close relationships," Victor observes.

Dr. Ken Lewis, director of Child Custody Services of Philadelphia and author of *Child Custody Litigation*, agrees. "While the inherent rights of grandparents should be a guiding principle, I feel there is a far more important right. This is the *implicit* right of the child as it is written in the First Amendment—the freedom of association," says Dr. Lewis. "To breech this role upon divorce is to make a separate class of children of divorce as opposed to an intact family."

Lewis's belief is that the courts should take the broadest approach possible, for many members of the extended family may or should have visitation rights. In some states these are called partial custody rights. "Of course," he adds, "they must be qualified to add to the life of the child. The courts still need to apply the doctrine of what is in the best interest of the child."

"I look at the bond that started *before* the separation or divorce," adds Dr. Lewis. He will spend a hundred hours or more with a client and hold in-depth interviews on the intimacy of the relationship between the grandparent and grandchild. If the grandchild is under six, he will observe who initiates contact and conversation. He will observe the child's behavior in reaching out, touching, going toward, or speaking to the grandparent. If the child is over six, Dr. Lewis will do all of the above as well as conduct interviews to determine the child's feelings toward the grandparent or any other extended family member who is seeking visitation or custody rights.

William B. Smith, a Virginia family law practitioner, adheres to the principle that grandparent visitation should be stipulated in a divorce agreement and should be part of the negotiated settlement. Many times, he claims, the court will appoint a guardian ad litem (who can be a lawyer or any other responsible person) to protect the interest of the child. This is done, he says, most often when litigation is contested. Smith sees an increase in court-ordered mediation in these types of cases and feels that mediation is helpful and works in almost every case. He notes that when the custodial parent is the mother, which is usually the case, she often tries to limit the father's visitation. And often what comes about is the narrowing of visitation by the paternal grandparents, and the relationship between these grandparents and the grandchild suffers.

Both Dr. Lewis and Smith share the view that having insufficient funds to hire an attorney should not stop you from asserting your grandparent rights. Smith says, "See the clerk of the court. Talk to him or her about filing a petition for visitation. The clerks are usually quite accessible and agreeable in helping a litigant, especially when they see you are trying to accomplish this on your own."

Smith notes that visitation is always open and negotiable. It can be changed later if deemed insufficient. He adds that you are more effective in these matters, however, with legal representation. And in custody disputes, it is really essential to have counsel, he warns.

"I have been known to deny significant visitation in what I call the 'divorce war,'" says Judge Lawrence L. Koontz, Jr. (Judge Koontz is a judge of the Court of Appeals of Virginia.) "When a grandparent continues to convey to the children that 'one of your parents is at fault and that you are sad and unhappy and being hurt by this parent'—well, then, if this grandparent cannot get above the fray, then I have to curtail this visitation. Sometimes I have had to use supervised visitation or severely limit visitation for grandparents. I have even ordered therapy for grandparents, as well as parents, when needed."

Virginia attorney Paul M. Lipkin, who specializes in family law, recalls judges restricting grandparental visitation when the grandparent appears to be exacerbating the rift between the parents. "In some situations," declares Lipkin, "I have witnessed judges ordering gradual visitation, such as starting with an hour a week, then adding two, and working up to a day, et cetera, when grandparents magnify problems in a divided family." Like Smith, this experienced family law practitioner suggests to grandparents that visitation with their grandchildren be spelled out in the divorce decree, especially if there is any type of controversy or animosity between the parties.

An unabashed believer in grandparents, Judge Koontz is acutely aware that a close relationship between grandparent and grandchild is *not* being divorced and should be preserved. "As children lose the continuity of their original family life, grandparents play an even more important part in the lives of these grandchildren. I believe that children have the right to grandparenting. There is the right to know your roots, whatever they are," explains Judge Koontz.

As a possible prerequisite to visitation, Judge Koontz addresses the grandparents' involvement. "What courts should do is look at what the family structure was 'in the good times'—before the breakup. What role did the grandparents play in these good times prior to the breakup of this family? But let me say this: Even if the grandparents had not been active before this crisis, this is not to say that they could not step forward at this juncture and be involved."

Judge Koontz states that when you are talking about the sensitivities of a family breakup and what is in the best interest of children, the adversarial system is by no means the best approach. The judge predicts that mediation will be more common in the future.

Attorney Paul Lipkin is sympathetic to the cause of mediation, declaring that it is far less adversarial. "Mediation," he says, "tries to get people to agree to certain things in the best interest of the child. Some states require mandatory mediation for all visitation and custody matters and utilize the mediation services and social workers within the court system. The judge often relies upon social services to do a home study and get a background report in about 80 percent of these cases. This report then gives the judge some insight into the relationship between the grandchild, grandparent, and parents."

Adoption and Visitation

Many states have enacted two grandparent visitation statutes: one for regular visitation, and the other for visitation after adoption. Much of the controversy revolves around whether adoption of a grandchild terminates or precludes a grandparental visitation order.

The courts have not conclusively addressed the question of whether adoption by a stepparent should be treated any differently than adoption by a nonrelative or a stranger.

Typically the grandparent visitation statutes permit grandparents to seek visitation in specified situations, but often these laws are silent on how adoption affects visitation rights. Courts are asked whether the termination of legal relationships upon adoption includes a termination of a natural grandparent's right to seek visitation.

Approximately twenty-three states now address the adoption issue in their grandparent visitation statutes. The majority of state statutes, however, are still vague as to the interplay of visitation and adoption law.

Most states permit grandparent visitation over the adoptive parent's objection and do not find this to be an unconstitutional impingement on the integrity of the adoptive family. Throughout court opinions one finds language such as: "The state, in its role as *parens patriae*, has determined that under certain circumstances, grandparents should have continuing contacts with the child's development if it is in the child's best interest. By enacting the visitation statute, the legislature has recognized that, particularly where a relationship between the grandparents and grandchild has been established, the child should not undergo the added burden of being severed from his or her grandparents, who may also provide the natural warmth, interest and support that will alleviate the child's misery."

Several appellate courts have held that grandparents have a right to intervene in an adoption case involving their grandchild. Such intervention may be particularly important to grandparents if their right to visit would be terminated upon adoption. It should be noted, however, that grandparental consent is *never* required as a prerequisite to an adoption.

A current problem is that most state statutes do not address such important procedural issues as whether grandparents must be notified of court proceedings directly affecting their grandchildren or themselves. Do grandparents have the right to intervene in proceedings affecting the custody and legal status of their grand-children? With the increasing volume of litigation regarding grandparent visitation, courts are now being asked such procedural questions. These questions are important because the answers may determine whether a grandparent will have an opportunity for a meaningful relationship with a grandchild.

CUSTODY

Conventional wisdom has it that when it comes to custody, no one is better able than a parent to decide what is best for a child. How-ever, changes in the American family over the last few decades have ravaged the traditional nuclear family. Increasingly, grand-parents have been left to raise children after the divorce of the natural parents. Grandparents have had to assume responsibility of parenting without protection that will allow them to continue the relationship should the biological parent later want the child back.

The California courts, in accordance with the "best interest" theory, have prioritized the awarding of custody as follows: (1) to both parents jointly or to either parent; (2) to the person or persons in whose home the child has been living in a wholesome and stable environment; (3) to any other person or persons deemed by the court to be suitable and able to provide adequate and proper care and guidance for the child.

Presently, the broadest statute pertaining to third-party custody is found in Hawaii. "Custody may be awarded to persons other than the father or mother whenever this award serves the best interest of the child. Any person who has had de facto custody of the child in a stable and wholesome home and is a fit and proper person shall prima facie be entitled to an award of custody."

In Mississippi, the law provides that "upon a finding by the

court that both of the parents of the child have abandoned or de-
serted such child or that both of such parents are mentally, morally
or otherwise unfit to rear and train the child, the court may award
physical and legal custody to a person deemed by the court to be
suitable and able to provide adequate and proper care and guidance
for the child."

The current laws in most of the fifty states advocate that when
there has been a prolonged separation from the child's custodial
parent and a strong attachment to another caretaker has evolved,
the state may legitimately seek to avoid emotional harm resulting
from severing ties with the primary caretaker (usually the grandparent).

Judge Koontz asserts that the courts go into different gear when
talking about taking children from their natural parents:

> The hardest case in my experience is where the grandparents come
> in and make all these sacrifices and rescue the child, and now they
> are told, with a stroke of a pen, "your turn is over." With time, I
> have seen more and more grandparents coming forward to challenge
> custody of their grandchildren (and to seek greater visitation). Some-
> times they admit to me that their own son or daughter is incapable of
> parenting due to drug or alcohol abuse or a general lack of commit-
> ment to the child. But we leave the door open, of course, for "a
> change of circumstance ruling" when we give the parent another
> chance or a trial period. The goal of the court is to restore custody
> to one of the natural parents whenever possible.

Attorney Paul Lipkin reflects on custody: "What is the criteria
for the grandparent, set forth by the courts, when the custodial
parent is deemed incompetent and the other parent is disengaged?
Basically the courts look at the desire, capability, and the health of
the grandparent."

Tazewell T. Hubard III, a mediator and family law specialist,
talks of a study made some years ago that addresses the factors that

enter into judicial decision making as to custody. (There were about twenty different categories, says Hubard.) About fifth on the list of importance is the availability and access of grandparents. "The courts have always looked to the role of grandparents and the wisdom of grandparents," claims Hubard. "When I mediate with a couple who is divorcing, I try and bring in the grandparents, if not physically. We discuss the access of these grandparents for the children—where they live and what support do these children have from them. Long-distance visitation is built into the divorce agreement."

Hubard capsulizes situations whereby grandparents may be awarded custody of their grandchildren, either temporarily or permanently:

If both parents are unable to function as parents, either because of alcohol or drug abuse, violence of any form, etc., grandparents can petition the court for temporary custody. For example, I had a case where a father had left and the mother was a drug addict. The children had no business living with the mother. There were capable grandparents around. I made the courts mindful of this fact. Of course, there is always a custody investigation and an at-home study that the court orders before children are placed with grandparents or any third party. There are checks and balances.

An article in *U.S. News & World Report* entitled "The Silent Saviors" declared in 1991 that 3.2 million children in the United States live with their grandparents. This is an astonishing increase of 40 percent in the last decade, according to the 1990 U.S. Census figures. Sylvie de Toledo, the executive director of an organization called Grandparents as Parents, admits that this tidal wave of grandparental custody is caused not just by the disruptive influence of divorce but also in large part by parents' drug and/or alcohol abuse and lack of commitment to the child. (De Toledo and Deborah E. Brown are coauthors of the book *Grandparents as Parents*.)

The Legal Rights of Grandparents

GENERAL CRITERIA FOR DETERMINING
VISITATION AND CUSTODY

As we have seen, in most states the standard for determining whether a court should award visitation or custody to grandparents is "what is in the best interests of the child." Although more than forty state statutes identify the "best interest" test as the guidepost for this type of decision making, very few state statutes articulate the specific criteria for determining this "best interest." In general, most state courts will be taking into consideration:

❧ Whether the child has lived with the grandparents and the length of that residence.

❧ Whether the grandparents have stood *in loco parentis* to the child. (*In loco parentis* means standing in the place of a parent and assuming the parent's rights, duties, and responsibilities.)

❧ The effect on the child's physical and emotional health of visitation or lack of it.

❧ The circumstances that resulted in the absence of a nuclear family.

❧ Where applicable, the child's preference regarding the visitation.

❧ The length and quality of the relationship between the grandparents and child.

❧ The child's need for continuity in relationships with people who may have played a significant nurturing role in his or her life.

❧ The effect of the termination of the child's relationship with the parent who has relinquished his or her rights and responsibilities (in cases of adoption, for example).

§ Whether friction between parent and grandparent has the potential for devastating consequences for the child. If so, grandparental visitation is deemed *not* to be in the child's best interest. In denying visitation to grandparents, the court looks to the record of evidence of severe ill feelings, bitterness, and animosity between the parties. In addition, the court determines whether the children show signs of stress before and after visits with these grandparents.

§ The recommendation regarding visitation made by any guardian ad litem who has been appointed to look after the interest of the child.

CHANGING THE LAWS

"It's only just beginning now," says Marian Robitaille. "Lawyers, judges, and the social service people are realizing the attachment of grandparents for grandchildren." Marian and her husband started a support group in their home. "We compared notes and cried on each other's shoulders," they report. "We contacted national grandparent groups for advice and assistance."

Over five hundred grandparents during the past twenty years have contacted Marian for advice and help in locating their grandchildren.

Although Marian and her husband were not successful in locating their twin grandsons, who are now nineteen years old, she continues to keep up the special journal she has written in since day one of this wrenching experience. "I write my thoughts and prayers from time to time about not being an active part of the boys' life and what we wish for our grandsons. I hope and pray that they know how much we love them and have always loved them. Maybe this journal or diary will get to them one day—perhaps after we're gone."

Initially, the Missing Children Help Center (a national organization) helped the Robitailles track down the boys. But just as soon as they were able to make a connection, the ex-daughter-in-law, new husband, and children moved again. Marian bemoans the fact that in the late 1970s and early 1980s, grandparents were not listened to very much in hearings and other court proceedings. Trying to locate their grandsons was a costly procedure, according to Marian, and they finally exhausted their funds.

As head of United Grandparents for Family Life (a Virginia organization; see appendix A), Marian can attest to the need for a national clearinghouse for grandparents at little or no cost to grandparents. "Most grandparents don't have much money. Most of us are living on retirement income and can't spend our life savings on lawyers," observes Robitaille. "I read about the progress that grandparents are now making all over the country in asserting their rights to see their grandchildren. I do think, however, that mediation is the way to go in matters like these. All the parties should sit down and agree on what is in the best interest of the grandchildren."

Because of the Robitailles' ordeal, Marian contacted her local legislative representative, and she and her husband focused attention on this issue through articles in local newspapers, in newsletters of grandparents' rights organizations, and through appearances on local TV and radio talk shows. Eventually, the Robitailles were able to apply enough pressure to improve and liberalize the grandparent statute in Virginia.

One voice *can* make a difference! Here are six steps you can take to make your voice heard:

1. If you are dissatisfied with your state's laws on any aspect of grandparenting, contact the office of your representative to the state legislature. If you don't know how to get in touch with him or her, or who is representing you in your district, or you do not know what district you reside in, call the Voter Regis-

trar's office in your community. From your address alone, the registrar can determine who is your representative to the state legislature, his or her business address, and office phone number. Or contact the reference department of your main library or call your city council. Some communities have a hot line when the legislature is in session, whereas others have an Office of Information.

2. You may also want to consider writing a letter to the committee or subcommittee that handles family issues in your legislature. In some states it is called the Committee of Courts and Justice or the Committee for Family Law. States use various names for such committees and subcommittees.

3. When the legislature is in session, get a group of grandparents together who have similar problems, and find out in advance when the committee or subcommittee is meeting. Ask for permission to be heard; you usually have to do this in advance in order to reserve a certain number of minutes to speak. You would be well served to prepare a brief outline of what you and your group hope to accomplish. Have additional copies of your remarks to distribute to each committee member and to members of the press. (Sometimes committee members are absent because they are voting in other committee hearings. Leave a copy of your remarks for any absent members, so they can read them at a later date.)

4. You may also wish to contact your state bar association and ask for the name of the chairman of the Family Law Section and each committee member's name and office address. Write each member, and get other interested grandparents to do the same. There is power in numbers!

5. See if there are any state organizations for grandparents in your area, or write one or more of the national organizations listed in appendix A. They may give you pointers on organizing

and lobbying your legislature. Or one of their well-versed members may even appear with you to reinforce your clout!

6. If your grandparent story is particularly heartbreaking, try to make contact with a member of the press. Newspaper reporters are always on the lookout for good human interest stories. The more exposure your dilemma receives, the better chance you have to reach the eyes and ears of the legislature and to thus enact change.

Although united grandparents have besieged their legislatures with requests to pass laws giving them the right to visit with their grandchildren, the response from the states has not been uniform. Grandparents who have been denied access to their grandchildren decry the lack of appropriate legislation necessary to *enforce* visitation. What is needed, say these grandparents, are uniform and reciprocal laws protecting the rights of grandparents and grandchildren.

Most legal practitioners attest to the fact that our laws should begin to reflect a more universal approach. Our laws vary widely from state to state—sometimes within a single state—as does the willingness to legislate and enforce third-party rights to children.

Yet family law, like other areas of the law, is in the process of becoming more national. Congressional involvement in spousal and child support (and its enforcement) is evidence of this new trend. Those in the child behavioral sciences and in the legal fields predict that over the next several decades we will come closer to a national consensus on third-party rights of other people's children. It is an issue crossing state lines and boundaries, with our grandchildren often residing in different states from where we, the grandparents, live.

With the increasing volume of litigation over grandparent visitation, court observers are also beginning to question if there is sufficient protection of due process for grandparents. Most state statutes do not appear to address such important procedural issues. Are grandparents in your state, for example, notified of court proceedings directly affecting their grandchildren or themselves? Do you have a right, as a grandparent, to intervene in any legal proceeding that directly affects the custody and legal status of your grandchildren? In addition, the majority of state statutes are still vague about the interplay of visitation by grandparents and adoption laws.

Former congressman Mario Biaggi (D-N.Y.), chairman of the House Human Services' Subcommittee of the Select Committee on Aging, held a public hearing in 1982 to focus national attention on the problems grandparents were having in obtaining visitation rights with their grandchildren. As a result of these hearings, a House Congressional Resolution was unanimously approved by the House. The congressional legislation noted the need for legislation to protect grandparents' rights and suggested that a uniform state act be developed and adopted by the states that would provide grandparents with the right to petition for visitation with their grandchildren following the dissolution of the marriage of their grandchildren's parents. The model act was also to provide grandparents visitation following a parent's remarriage and a stepparent's adoption of a grandchild. However, as of this date—twelve years later—the National Conference of Commissioners on Uniform State Laws has not developed such a model state act.

Currently, the issue of grandparents' rights is under the aegis of the United States Senate Special Committee on Aging, with Senator David Pryor (D-Ark.) at its helm. According to Holly Bode, staff person to the senator, this committee will be focusing national attention on expanding grandparents' rights.

But for the most part, Bode contends, it will be left to the states to deal with these matters since the states handle the divorce decree and all custody and visitation matters therein. However, Bode characterizes the Senate Special Committee on Aging as being charged with the development of a Grandparent Bill of Rights.

Senator Pryor's committee, Bode explains, seeks to raise the consciousness of the American public about the innumerable aspects of today's grandparenting role and the contribution grandparents are making in the lives of their grandchildren.

In the meanwhile, grandparents' rights organizations continue to argue for a national clearinghouse for grandparents, whereby grandparents may try to locate their grandchildren. Other grandparents decry the need for court-ordered mediation in disputes involving the rights of grandchildren with their grandparents in both visitation and custody disputes. Grandparents who have been involved in costly litigation, and the legal entanglements that ensue, advocate a stronger alternative method for dispute resolution—a turning away from the adversarial approach. As one grandparent has observed, "We need to establish national standards for grandparents and grandchildren who have been deprived of one another's love and affection."

7.

New Family Constellations

§

YOUR ROLE

AS A STEPGRANDPARENT

It's possible that your son or daughter will remarry at some time in the future. This development will require many changes and adjustments for both your adult child and your grandchildren. (There's enough material here for a whole new book.) The marriage may also give you some relatives you hadn't counted on: stepgrandchildren. Since the issue of stepgrandchildren is a difficult one for most grandparents, it will be the subject of this final chapter.

With half of all marriages ending in divorce and parents frequently remarrying to form new family constellations, many youngsters and oldsters must learn new roles as stepgrandchildren and stepgrandparents. Powerful changes have impacted on the grandparent-grandchild relationship. Each generation has much to give to the other, observes Dr. Mary Cerney, a former Menninger psychologist and psychoanalyst who frequently speaks on grandparenting issues.

Stepgrandchildren more often than not come into a blended family with a grandparent or two. With remarriage, some children may have as many as four sets of grandparents. And believe it or not, says Dr. Arthur Kornhaber, even with all of these grandparents around, many stepgrandchildren are still searching for quality grandparenting.

The Aring Institute offers the following guidelines for step-grandparents:

♦ Try to educate yourself about stepfamilies.

♦ Know each stepgrandchild as an individual.

♦ Give everybody time.

♦ Be sensitive to your stepgrandchild's change of status.

♦ Try to have a special place for your stepgrandchild's things at your home.

♦ Although you may never love your stepgrandchild, you can at least respect him or her.

♦ Since different grandparenting styles and family customs cause conflict, be *flexible* about your differences. Use humor and avoid quid pro quo (the old tit-for-tat routine).

♦ Seek out a professional or a good friend with a clear head if you need to talk things out.

♦ Do not be overly self-sacrificing; make sure you are yourself, too.

Remember that a stepchild has to deal with many changes. After a divorce and time alone with the single parent, this child must now adjust to remarriage, new people, new places, new emotions. There is now a new adult figure in the house, not to mention stepbrothers, sisters, and stepgrandparents. There are loyalty conflicts between new parents and old, moves to new homes and new schools, leaving old friends behind, a new financial status, and a reorganization of household routines.

So it is not surprising that your stepgrandchild feels high levels of stress. According to James Bray, a psychologist at Baylor College of Medicine, most of the problems mentioned are temporary: "Over time, things do seem to settle down."

As noted in the preceding guidelines, you may never love your stepgrandchildren. Or even like them as much as your own biological grandchildren. Psychotherapists say this is a very common issue among the families they see, although most grandparents heartily deny it.

One behaviorist notes that "stepgrandparents find their feelings toward their stepgrandchildren confusing. Many expect to have loving feelings automatically and instantly toward the stepgrandchildren. This is quite unrealistic."

As one stepgrandmother remembers: "I thought I would be able to love my daughter's stepson just because he was now a part of our family. But it didn't happen that way; there was no instant bonding. After some therapy, I was relieved of a lot of guilt. I was shown that it wasn't my feelings so much as my actions and attitudes toward him that mattered."

Relating to a teenage stepgrandchild can be especially difficult. The stepgrandparent may not like the teen's looks, personality, style of dress, speech, or choice of friends. Without a shared heritage and common family memories, it's harder to deal with these negative impressions.

One stepgrandmother explains how she and her husband developed a relationship with Tim, their fifteen-year-old stepgrandson:

We had to go back in time to when our own kids were teens and remember that it's only a stage. We reached out as much as we could—birthdays, holidays, family dinners. I think what helped the most, though, was the interest my husband showed toward Tim's love of basketball. They would sit for hours and watch college and pro games. My husband went to all of Tim's high school games and even gave him tips on the lay-up shot—the one our own son had perfected through my husband's guidance. In time we feel Tim looked upon us as good friends, if not exactly grandparents.

Although it is recognized that there may occasionally be a honeymoon period between stepgrandparents and stepgrandchildren because of the wonder of exploring a new relationship, the shared history between natural grandparents and their biological grandchildren all but guarantees a modicum of favoritism.

Those who practice in the mental health fields stress the importance of not comparing your natural grandchildren and stepgrandchildren. Instead, look for ways to recognize and show respect for your grandchildren's differences. This approach will not only increase their self-esteem, but also avoid the problems and expectations that come with attempts at identical treatment.

Sally Brush, director of the Aring Institute, notes that these grandchildren had no choice in the ending of their first family or in the forming of the new one. "They are feeling confused. They are both happy and angry about the remarriage," she explains. Stepfamilies have difficulties and differences to work through. "Presenting a polished picture to outsiders is not important," she observes. "The point . . . is that this new family will be neither better nor worse; it will simply be *different*." Brush goes on to say that

If the kids see you're interested in building relationships rather than wielding any type of authority or being competitive with the other grandparents, then this can be a tremendous advantage for them.

When stepgrandchildren find satisfaction and comfort in visiting with and relating to their new grandparents—where there is cooperation, flexibility, empathy, and responsiveness—there's a better

chance of building a strong, cohesive stepfamily. This can be an exciting opportunity for grandparents if they choose to take this path.

Treating children identically is an impossible task. Trying to do so, professionals assert, only encourages children to keep score and to seek out petty differences that they can use in arguments with their siblings or with you or their parents. Try not to "force-fit" your natural grandchild and stepgrandchild into an activity only one of them likes. Emphasize fairness. Giving one child a skateboard and another a pair of Rollerblades or giving one child piano lessons and another ballet lessons may make more sense.

Some stepgrandparents have problems with disciplining stepgrandchildren while they are under their care. One grandparent came up against the "poor little thing" syndrome, in which her stepgranddaughter had not been held accountable for negative behavior in a misguided attempt to make up for the painful realities in her life. The Stepfamily Association of America advises that grandparents should treat all grandchildren—natural, adopted, or step—*equally* in terms of rules, rewards, and responsibilities.

Just as your friendship with your natural grandchild develops faster from one-on-one interaction, stepgrandparents and stepgrandchildren need time alone together, even if it's spent just doing errands. And as several grandparents have demonstrated, sharing skills and talents is an excellent way to promote bonding. Teach your stepgrandchild how to garden or make spaghetti or play golf. When the natural parent or stepparent is at work, it means a lot to a child to have a grandparent around.

Other helpful hints are featured in *Step Kids (A Survival Guide for Teenagers in Stepfamilies)* by Ann Getzoff and Carolyn McClenahan. They are applicable to grandparents as well as to the teens and parents the book is intended for. Level with the children, step- or otherwise. Let them know how their behavior affects you. Often stepgrandchildren don't realize what things you may find irritating.

Above all, keep your promises, keep your grandchildren's confidences and secrets, and eliminate teasing about sensitive issues.

Presently, one in three Americans is a member of a stepfamily. This figure is expected to rise to nearly one in two by the turn of the century. Social legislation or profamily policies designed to reinforce only one model of the American family (i.e., the old "Ozzie and Harriet" version) are shortsighted and have the unintended consequence of weakening, rather than strengthening family ties.

Carol J. DeVita, a senior research demographer at the Population Reference Bureau, a private, nonprofit, Washington-based group, says, "It's a mistake for policy making in the United States to focus on the 'traditional family'! In doing that," DeVita claims, "you're leaving out a lot of other people. What we need to do is broaden our view of what the family is."

What is your definition of the American family? In a recent study on the American family and its values, *Life* magazine raised the question. Only 22 percent thought a family was "a group of people related by blood, marriage, or adoption." The definition preferred by 74 percent was much broader in its scope. "A family is a group of people who love and care for one another" was the majority view.

Life magazine's writers have their own definition of family: "Its existence is an inspiration for our greatest acts of love, our worst nightmares, our finest dreams. The family is a living, pulsing organism, continually changing and continually reinventing itself."

So it appears that we grandparents also have some fine-tuning to do in order that we may reinvent ourselves as well. Along the way we must find guidelines for inclusiveness instead of exclusivity about what "family" is all about.

Appendix A

RESOURCES FOR GRANDPARENTS' NETWORKING

American Bar Association
Commission on Legal Problems for the Elderly
Naomi Karp, Staff Attorney
1800 M. Street, N.W.
Washington, DC 20036
202-331-2297

Association of Family and Conciliation Courts
Victoria Metz, Office Manager
329 W. Wilson Street
Madison, Wisconsin 53703

Beech Acres' Aring Institute
(a divorce clinic)
Sally Brush, Executive Director
6881 Beechmont Avenue
Cincinnati, Ohio 45230
513-231-6630

Foundation for Grandparenting
Dr. Arthur Kornhaber, President
Carol M. Kornhaber, Executive Director
Box 31
Lake Placid, New York 12946
518-523-1825
315-354-5311 (for grandparent-grandchild summer camp)

Grandparents
Scarsdale Family Counseling Service
405 Harwood Building
Scarsdale, New York 10583
914-723-3281

Grandparents as Parents
Sylvie de Toledo, Executive Director
11260 Overland Avenue, 17D
Culver City, California 90230
310-924-3996

Grandparents/Childrens' Rights
Lee and Lucille Sumpter
5728 Bayonne Avenue
Haslett, Michigan 28840
517-339-8663
(The Sumpters will put you in touch with your state leader.)

Grandparents Rights Organization
Richard S. Victor, Executive Director
555 S. Woodward
Suite 600
Birmingham, Michigan 48009
313-646-7191
Fax 313-646-9722

Grandparents United for Children's Rights, Inc.
Ethel Dunn, Executive Director
137 Larkin Street
Madison, Wisconsin 53705
608-238-8751

Missing Children Help Center
410 Ware Boulevard
Suite 400
Tampa, Florida 33619
813-623-KIDS
800-USA-KIDS

National Council of Children's Rights
Strengthening Families and Assisting
Children of Separation and Divorce
David Levy, President
220 I. Street, N.W.
Suite 230
Washington, DC 20002
202-547-NCCR

Appendix A

Scarsdale Family Counseling Service
Grandparent Support Group
Edith S. Engel, Coleader
10 Gerlach Place
Larchmont, New York 10538
914-834-5510

United Grandparents for Family Life (Virginia only)
Marion Robitaille, Leader
5243 Lepage Road
Norfolk, Virginia 23513
804-855-6844

Appendix B

STATUTES ON GRANDPARENTS' VISITATION

All fifty states now have laws dealing with the issue of grandparents and grandchildren and their right to visit and communicate with one another. Some states include other interested third parties, as well. These state laws appear to fall into three categories:

1. Laws that provide for reasonable visitation rights of maternal or paternal grandparents with no prerequisites.

2. Laws that grant visitation rights of grandparents only if there has been a death, divorce, or stepparent adoption.

3. Laws that now have opened the door to grandparents to request visitation of grandchildren, as well as to any other person who has an interest in the child.

A *caveat for the reader*: Statutory laws can evolve and change rapidly. So it may behoove you to check the appropriate statute number and its modification, if any, applicable to visitation.

The following listing of state-by-state laws regarding grandparent visitation rights was excerpted from the periodical *Divorce Litigation*, vol. 4, no. 12 (December 1992), published by the National Legal Research Group. The entry for each state includes the statute number and type, and, where illuminating, a representative case in the jurisdiction interpreting the statute.

Alabama. Ala. Code §§30-3-4 (1989), 26-10A-30 (1992): grant visitation on death of parent, on divorce of parents, where grandparent has been unreasonably denied visitation for 90 days, and on adoption of child. *Mills v. Parker*, 549 So.2d 97 (Ala. Civ. App. 1989) (court has jurisdiction to entertain grandparent visitation petition whenever there has been a disruption in the family); *Ex parte Palmer*, 574 So.2d 44 (Ala. 1990) (circuit court was court in which petition for visitation might be heard).

Alaska. Alaska Stat. §25–24.150 (1991): grants visitation on death of parent and on divorce of parents.

Arizona. Ariz. Rev. Stat. Ann. §25.377.01 (Supp. 1992): grants visitation on death of parent, where parent is declared missing, on divorce of parents, where child is born out of wedlock, and where parental rights have been terminated. Visitation rights are automatically terminated upon adoption. *Sands* v. *Sands*, 157 Ariz. 322, 757 P.2d 126 (Ct. App. 1988).

Arkansas. Ark. Code Ann. §9–13–103 (Michie 1991): grants visitation on death of parent and on divorce of parents. *Sanders* v. *Sanders*, 297 Ark. 621, 764 S.W.2d 443 (1989) (grandparents may bring their own action for visitation, and need not join in divorce action); *Rudolph* v. *Floyd*, 309 Ark. 514, 832 S.W.2d 219 (1992) (paternity adjudication gave grandparent of child born out of wedlock right to petition for visitation with child).

California. Cal. Civ. Code §197.5 (West 1982), §§4601, 4351.1 (West Supp. 1992): grant visitation on death of parent and on divorce of parents. *White* v. *Jacobs*, 198 Ca. App.3d 122, 243 Cal. Rptr. 597 (1988) (grandparents do not have the right to petition for visitation while nuclear family is intact); *accord In re Marriage of Gayden*, 229 Cal. App.3d 1510, 280 Cal. Rptr. 862 (1991).

Colorado. Colo. Rev. Stat. §19–1–117 (Supp. 1992): grants visitation on death of parent, on divorce of parents, and where parental rights have been terminated. *People in Interest of N.S.*, 821 P.2d 931 (Colo. Ct. App. 1991) (grandparent has right to petition for visitation during dependency hearing, but adoption of child will terminate visitation rights).

Connecticut. Conn. Gen. Stat. Ann. §46b–59 (West 1986): grants visitation with no prerequisites. *Lehrer* v. *Davis*, 214 Conn. 232, 571 A.2d 691 (1990) (statute did not impermissibly interfere with the parents' right to raise their children as they saw fit).

Delaware. Del. Code Ann. tit. 10, §950(7) (Supp. 1992): grants visitation with no prerequisites, but prohibits order of visitation if both parents object while they cohabit as husband and wife.

Florida. Fla. Stat. Ann. §§61.13, 752.01 (West Supp. 1991): grant visitation on death of parent, on divorce of parents, where child has been adopted by step-parent, and where child is born out of wedlock. *Sketo* v. *Brown*, 559 So.2d 381 (Fla. Dist. Ct. App. 1990) (statute was facially valid because the state had a compelling interest in the welfare of the children). *Compare Hern-*

don v. *Herndon*, 575 So.2d 792 (Fla. Dist. Ct. App. 1991) (court has jurisdiction to enter orders where there was a pending action between husband and wife) *with Sragowicz* v. *Sragowicz*, 603 So.2d 1323 (Fla. Dist. Ct. App. 1992) (court no longer had jurisdiction to order grandparent visitation once underlying divorce action was dismissed).

Georgia. Ga. Code Ann. §§19–7–3, 19–8–13, 19–9–3 (Michie 1991): grant visitation on death of parent and on divorce of parents. Adoption cuts off all relations between child and grandparents. *Anderson* v. *Sanford*, 198 Ga. App. 40, 401 S.E.2d 604 (1991) (right of grandparents to intervene in deprivation action did not bar their subsequent right to file an original petition for visitation).

Hawaii. Haw. Rev. Stat. §571–46 (7) (Supp. 1991): grants visitation where there is a dispute as to custody.

Idaho. Idaho Code §32–1008 (1983): grants visitation with no prerequisites.

Illinois. Ill. Ann. Stat. ch.40, ¶607(b), (c) (Smith-Hurd Supp. 1992), ch. 110, ¶11–7.1 (Smith-Hurd Supp. 1992): grant visitation on death of parent and on divorce of parents. *Lingwall* v. *Hoener*, 108 Ill.2d 206, 483 N.E.2d 512 (1985) (court should consider parents' attitude toward visitation, quality and length of grandparent/grandchild relationship, and child's need for continuity in relationships); *accord McVey* v. *Frederickson*, 226 Ill. App.3d 1082, 590 N.E.2d 996 (1992).

Indiana. Ind. Code Ann. §§31–1–11.7–2 *et seq.* (Burns 1987 & Supp. 1991): grant visitation on death of parent, on divorce of parents, where child is born out of wedlock, and on termination of parental rights. *Bailey* v. *Menzie*, 542 N.E.2d 1015, 1020 (Ind. Ct. App. 1989) (Indiana's Act interferes with a parent's liberty interests only to observe its duty under the *parens patriae* doctrine and only upon a finding that it would be in the best interests of the child; the General Assembly has employed means reasonably related to a legitimate end of state government). N.B.: The Indiana statute has been amended since the decision of *Bailey* v. *Menzie*, *supra*, for its well-reasoned discussion of constitutional concerns. *See also Lockhart* v. *Lockhart*, 19 Fam. L. Rep. (BNA) 1071 (Ind. Ct. App. 1992) (parents of spouse who has been awarded primary physical custody of children in divorce action may not seek visitation; grandparents cannot seek visitation against wishes of their own child).

Iowa. Iowa Code Ann. §598.35 (West Supp. 1992): grants visitation on death of parent, on divorce of parents, where child is born out of wedlock, and where parental rights have been terminated.

Kansas. Kan. Stat. Ann. §§60–1616(b) (1987), 38–129 (Supp. 1991): grant visitation on divorce of parents and in any custody matter before the court. *Spradling* v. *Harris,* 13 Kan. App.2d 595, 778 P.2d 365 (1989) (under doctrine of *parens patriae,* state may validly order visitation where it is in the best interests of the child).

Kentucky. Ky. Rev. Stat. Ann. §405.021 (Michie 1984): grants visitation with no prerequisites. *King* v. *King,* 828 S.W.2d 630 (Ky.), *cert. denied,* 113 S. Ct. 378 (1992) (few would dispute that there are great benefits to be derived from the establishment of a bond between grandparent and grandchild; court is thus invested with power pursuant to statute to grant visitation when it is in the best interests of the child).

Louisiana. La. Rev. Stat. Ann. §9:572 (West 1991); La. Children's Code Ann. art. 1264 (1992): grants visitation on death of parent, on divorce of parents, and where parental rights have been terminated. *McCarty* v. *Mc-Carty,* 559 So.2d 517 (La. Ct. App. 1990) (grandparent visitation may be granted only in those circumstances contained in statute).

Maine. Me. Rev. Stat. Ann. tit. 19, §§752(6), 1001 *et seq.* (West Supp. 1992): grant visitation on divorce and on death of parent.

Maryland. Md. Fam. Law Code Ann. §9–102 (1991): grants visitation on death of parent and on divorce of parents. *Skeens* v. *Paterno,* 60 Md. App. 48, 480 A.2d 820, *cert. denied,* 301 Md. 689, 484 A.2d 274 (1984) (court may grant petition for grandparent visitation where child is born out of wedlock).

Massachusetts. Mass. Gen. Laws Ann. ch. 119, §39D (West Supp. 1992): grants visitation on death of parents and on divorce of parents, and where child is born out of wedlock; prohibits visitation after adoption of child. *Adoption & Visitation of a Minor,* 14 Mass. App. Ct. 992, 440 N.E.2d 766 (1982).

Michigan. Mich. Comp. Laws Ann. §772.27b (West Supp. 1992); Mich. Stat. Ann. §25–312(7b) (Law. Co-op. Supp. 1992): grant visitation on death of parent, on divorce of parents, and where parental rights have been termi-nated. *Ruppel* v. *Lesner,* 421 Mich. 559, 364 N.W.2d 665 (1985) (grand-parents may not petition for visitation while nuclear family is intact); *accord Nelson* v. *Kendrick,* 187 Mich. App. 367, 466 N.W.2d 402 (1991); *see also Brown* v. *Brown,* 192 Mich. App. 44, 480 N.W.2d 292 (1991) (grandparent visitation that may be granted in "child custody dispute" includes annulment of marriage and other marriage-related actions).

Appendix B

Minnesota. Minn. Stat. Ann. §257.022 (West Supp. 1992): grants visitation on death of parent, on divorce of parents, and after living with grandparent. Prohibits visitation after adoption. *In re Welfare of R.A.N.*, 435 N.W.2d 71 (Minn. Ct. App. 1989).

Mississippi. Miss. Code Ann. §§93–16–1 *et seq.* (Supp. 1992): grant visitation on death of parent, on divorce of parents, and where parental rights have been terminated. Prohibits visitation after adoption. *In re Adoption of a Minor*, 558 So.2d 854 (Miss. 1990).

Missouri. Mo. Ann. Stat. §452.402 (Vernon Supp. 1992): grants visitation on death of parent and on divorce of parents; also grants visitation to grandparent where grandparent has been unreasonably denied visitation. Grandparent visitation does not terminate upon termination of parental rights. *Farrell* v. *Denson*, 821 S.W.2d 547 (Mo. Ct. App. 1991) (where statute provides that court may grant grandparent visitation where grandparent has been unreasonably denied visitation for 90 days, 90 days refers to period before court makes its order, not period before application for visitation is filed); *In re CER*, 796 S.W.2d 423 (Mo. Ct. App. 1990) (grandparents may petition for visitation of child born out of wedlock).

Montana. Mont. Code Ann. §§40–9–101 *et seq.* (1991): grant visitation with no prerequisites. Prohibit visitation after adoption.

Nebraska. Neb. Rev. Stat. §§43–1801 *et seq.* (1988): grant visitation on death of parent, on divorce of parents, and on adjudication of paternity of child born out of wedlock.

Nevada. Nev. Rev. Stat. Ann. §§125A:330, 125A:340 (Michie Supp. 1991): grant visitation on death of parent and on divorce of parents.

New Hampshire. N.H. Rev. Stat. Ann. §458:17–d (1992): grants visitation on death of parent, on divorce of parent, on adoption by a stepparent, and where child is born out of wedlock. *Preston* v. *Mercieri*, 133 N.H. 36, 573 A.2d 128 (1990) (while recognizing constitutional interests of parents, court has power, under doctrine of *parens patriae*, to order grandparent visitation whenever best interests of child so dictate, not only when parents are divorced or the nuclear family has otherwise been disrupted; thus, statute will be interpreted to grant visitation when such is in the best interests of the child).

New Jersey. N.J. Stat. Ann. §9–2–7.1 (West Supp. 1992): grants visitation on death of parent and on divorce of parents. *Thompson* v. *Vanaman*, 212 N.J.

Super. 596, 515 A.2d 1254 (App. Div. 1986) (grandparents may not petition for visitation while nuclear family is intact).

New Mexico. N.M. Stat. Ann. §§40–9–1 *et seq.* (Michie 1989): grant visitation on death of parent, on divorce, after living with grandparent, and where paternity has been established. *Christian Placement Service* v. *Gordon,* 102 N.M. 465, 697 P.2d 148 (Ct. App. 1985) (grandparent visitation may not be granted after parental rights have been terminated by adoption).

New York. N.Y. Dom. Rel. Law §§72, 240 (McKinney Supp. 1992): grant visitation on death of parent, on divorce of parents, and where "equity would intervene" to grant such visitation. *Sibley* v. *Sheppard,* 54 N.Y.2d 320, 445 N.Y.S.2d 420, 423 (1981) (statute does not unconstitutionally infringe upon parent's right to raise child). *But see Emanuel S.* v. *Joseph E.,* 161 A.D.2d 83, 560 N.Y.S.2d 211 (1990) (court will not intervene absent extraordinary circumstances, such as disintegration of nuclear family).

North Carolina. N.C. Gen. Stat. §50–13.2(b1) (1987): grants visitation on divorce of parents only. *Moore* v. *Moore,* 89 N.C. App. 351, 365 S.E.2d 662 (1988) (grandparents may not petition for visitation while nuclear family is intact).

North Dakota. N.D. Cent. Code §14–09–05.1 (1991): grants visitation with no prerequisites. *Shempp-Cook* v. *Cook,* 455 N.W.2d 216 (N.D. 1990) (in determining the best interests of the child, the court must consider the ongoing relationship between the child and the third party, and whether visitation would interfere with the parent-child relationship).

Ohio. Ohio Rev. Code Ann. §§3109.051, 3109.11 (Anderson Supp. 1991): grant visitation on death of parent and on divorce of parents. *In re Gibson,* 61 Ohio St.3d 168, 573 N.E.2d 1074 (1991) (court may grant grandparent visitation only in those circumstances contained in statute).

Oklahoma. Okla. Stat. Ann. tit. 10 §§5,60.16 (West Supp. 1993): grant visitation with no prerequisites. *Ingram* v. *Ingram,* 814 P.2d 1052 (Okla. Ct. App. 1991) (considering high level of acrimony between third party and parent of child, court disinclined to order third-party visitation).

Oregon. Or. Rev. Stat. §§107.105(1)(b), 109.119 *et seq.* (1990): grants visitation with no prerequisites. *Machado* v. *Uri,* 94 Or. App. 731, 767 P.2d 106 (1989) (court must consider relationship between third party and child, preferences of child, and well-being of child). *But see In re Grant,* 114 Or. App.

549, 836 P.2d 167 (1992) (court may not order grandparent visitation after termination of parental rights).

Pennsylvania. Pa. Stat. Ann. tit. 23, §§5311 *et seq.* (1991): grant visitation on death of parent, on divorce of parents, and after living with grandparent. Visitation terminates on adoption by one other than stepparent or grandparent. *Johnson* v. *Deisenger,* 404 Pa. Super. 41, 589 A.2d 1160 (1991) (trial court must consider the physical, intellectual, emotional, and spiritual well-being of the child, and whether continuing an ongoing grandparent/grandchild relationship would serve those interests).

Rhode Island. R.I. Gen. Laws §§15–5–24.1 *et seq.* (1988): grant visitation with no prerequisites.

South Carolina. S.C. Code Ann. §20–7–420 (33) (Law. Co-op. 1985): grants visitation with no prerequisites.

South Dakota. S.D. Codified Laws Ann. §§25–5–52 *et seq.* (1992): grant visitation with no prerequisites. Any grandparent rights that may have been granted terminate upon the termination of parental rights. *Strousser* v. *Olson,* 397 N.W.2d 651 (S.D. 1986) (court would not order grandparent visitation where there was severe ill will among all parties, and children testified they did not wish to visit grandparents).

Tennessee. Tenn. Code Ann. §36–6–301 (1991): grants visitation with no prerequisites. *Clark* v. *Evans,* 778 S.W.2d 446 (Tenn. Ct. App. 1989) (the state has decided that the promotion of strong grandparent/grandchild bonds are to be favored, and this is a legitimate state end to promote); *see also Op. Att'y Gen. 91–21* (Mar. 7, 1991), given in response to *Hawk* v. *Hawk,* Docket No. 996, now pending before the Tennessee Supreme Court.

Texas. Tex. Fam. Code Ann. §14.03(e)–(g) (West Supp. 1993): grants visitation on death of parent, on divorce of parents, where parental rights have been terminated, and after living with grandparent. *Tope* v. *Kaminski,* 793 S.W.2d 315 (Tex. App. 1990).

Utah. Utah Code Ann. §30–5–2 (1991): grants visitation with no prerequisites. *Kasper* v. *Nordfelt,* 815 P.2d 747 (Utah Ct. App. 1991) (grandparent visitation statute does not apply where child has been adopted by one other than stepparent or grandparent).

Vermont. Vt. Stat. Ann. tit. 15, §§1011 *et seq.* (1989): grant visitation with no prerequisites. *In re S.B.L.,* 150 Vt. 294, 553 A.2d 1078 (1988) (grandparent visitation must expire on adoption by person other than stepparent or grandparent).

Virginia. Va. Code Ann. §20–107.2 (Michie 1991): grants visitation on divorce of parents only.

Washington. Wash. Rev. Code Ann. §26.09.240 (West Supp. 1992): grants visitation with no prerequisites. *Bond* v. *Yount,* 47 Wash. App. 181, 734 P.2d 39 (1987) (grandparents have no standing to petition for visitation where child has been adopted).

West Virginia. W. Va. Code Ann. §§48–2B–1 *et seq.* (Supp. 1992): grant visitation on death of parent, in divorce of parents, when child has resided with grandparents, and where child was born out of wedlock.

Wisconsin. Wis. Stat. Ann. §§767.245, 880.155 (West Supp. 1990): grant visitation with no prerequisites. *Van Cleve* v. *Hemminger,* 141 Wis.2d 543, 415 N.W.2d 571 (Ct. App.), *review denied,* 141 Wis.2d 985, 416 N.W.2d 297 (1987) (while statute provides no prerequisites to grandparent visitation, an order of visitation over the objection of parents in a still intact family violates the parents' Fourteenth Amendment liberty rights).

Wyoming. Wyo. Stat. §20–2–113(c) (Supp. 1992): grants visitation on divorce of parents or in any juvenile proceeding.

Bibliography

BOOKS

For Grandparents

Aldrich, Robert A., and Glenn Austin. *Grandparenting for the Nineties*. Escondido, Calif.: Robert Erdmann, 1991.

American Bar Association. *The Family Law Quarterly*, vol. 25, no. 1. (Special issue on third-party custody, visitation, and child support.) Chicago, 1991.

de Toledo, Sylvie, and Deborah Elder Brown. *Grandparents as Parents*. New York: Guilford Press, 1994.

Gardner, Richard A. *Family Evaluation in Child Custody: Mediation, Arbitration, and Litigation*. Cresskill, N.J.: Creative Therapeutics, 1989.

Keen, Sam. *Fire in the Belly*. New York: Bantam, 1991.

Kornhaber, Arthur, and Kenneth L. Woodward. *Grandparents/Grandchildren: The Vital Connection*. New Brunswick, N.J.: Transaction, 1985.

Lerner, Harriet Goldhor. *The Dance of Anger*. New York: Harper and Row, 1989.

LeShan, Eda. *Grandparenting in a Changing World*. New York: Newmarket Press, 1993.

Lewis, Karen Gail, ed. *Siblings in Therapy*. New York: Norton, 1988.

Lewis, Ken. *Child Custody Litigation*. Eclair, Wisconsin: National Business Institute, 1990. (For copies, write to Dr. Ken Lewis c/o Child Custody Services of Philadelphia, Inc., 2258 Menlo Avenue, Glenside, Pennsylvania 19038.)

Parker, Charles E. *Deep Recovery: How to Use Your Most Difficult Relationships to Find Out Who You Are*. Virginia Beach: Hawkeye, 1992.

Thompson, Mary. *Simply Christmas*. New York: Walker, 1992. (Gift ideas for Christmas and throughout the year.)

Warshak, Richard A. *The Custody Revolution: The Father Factor and the Motherhood Mystique*. New York: Poseidon, 1992.

Wasserman, Selma. *The Long-Distance Grandmother: How to Stay Close to Distant Children*. Point Roberts, Wash.: Hartley and Marks, 1990.

Wyse, Lois. *Grandchildren Are So Much Fun, I Should Have Had Them First.* New York: Crown, 1992.

For Grandparents and Grandchildren

Williamson Publishing, in Charlotte, Vermont, has a number of excellent and inexpensive paperback books that are filled with ideas for activities. These books cover a wide range of ages and interests, and include:

Carlson, Laurie. *Eco-Art: Earth-Friendly Art and Craft Experiences for Three- to Nine-Year-Olds.* Kids Can! Series. 1993.
———. *Kids Create: Art and Craft Experiences for Three- to Nine-Year-Olds.* Kids Can! Series. 1990.
Catchpole, Terry, and Catherine Catchpole. *The Family Video Guide: Over 300 Movies to Share with Your Children.* 1992.
Gordon, Patricia, and Reed C. Snow. *Kids Learn America: Bringing Geography to Life with People, Places, and History.* Kids Can! Series. 1991.
Hart, Avery, and Paul Mantell. *Kids and Weekends: Creative Ways to Make Special Days.* Kids Can! Series. 1992.
———. *Kids Make Music: Clapping and Tapping from Bach to Rock.* Kids Can! Series. 1993.
Jones, Claudia. *Parents Are Teachers, Too: Enriching Your Child's First Six Years.* 1988.
Milord, Susan. *Adventures in Art: Art and Craft Experiences for Seven- to Fourteen-Year-Olds.* Kids Can! Series. 1990.
———. *Hands Around the World: 365 Creative Ways to Build Cultural Awareness and Global Respect.* Kids Can! Series. 1992.
———. *The Kids' Nature Book: 365 Indoor/Outdoor Activities and Experiences.* Kids Can! Series. 1989.
Sonna, Linda A. *The Homework Solution: Getting Kids to Do Their Homework.* 1990.
Terzian, Alexandra M. *The Kids' Multicultural Art Book: Art and Craft Experiences from Around the World.* Kids Can! Series. 1993.
Williamson, Sarah, and Zachary Williamson. *Kids Cook: Fabulous Food for the Whole Family.* Kids Can! Series. 1992.

Other helpful books:

Brogan, John. *The Kid's Guide to Divorce.* New York: Fawcett Crest, 1986. (For teens.)

Bibliography

Lipson, Eden Ross. *The New York Times Parent's Guide to the Best Books for Children*. New York: Random House, 1991.

For Children in Stepfamilies

Berry, Joy. *Good Answers to Tough Questions About Stepfamilies*. Chicago: Children's Press, 1990.

Gardner, Richard A. *The Boys' and Girls' Book About Stepfamilies*. Cresskill, N.J.: Creative Therapeutics, 1985.

Getzoff, Ann, and Carolyn McClenahan. *Step Kids*. (*A Survival Guide for Teenagers in Stepfamilies*). New York: Walker, 1984.

Glassman, Bruce. *Everything You Need To Know About Step-families*. New York: Rosen Publishing Group, 1991. (For late elementary and teens.)

Noble, June. *Where Do I Fit In?* Austin, Tex.: Holt, Rinehart, & Winston, 1981. (Fiction for late elementary and teens.)

Roosevelt, Ruth, and Jeanette Lofas. *Living in Step*. New York: Stein and Day, 1976. (For teens.)

Sobol, Harriet L. *My Other—Mother, My Other—Father*. New York: Macmillan, 1979. (For ages eight to twelve.)

Wolkoff, Judie. *Happily Ever After. . . Almost*. New York: Dell Yearling, reissue 1984. (Fiction for ages eight to sixteen.)

ARTICLES

Boley, Carol Daniels. "When You're Mom No. 2." *Focus on the Family*, July 1989.

Cerney, Mary. "Accenting the Grand in Grandparenting." *The Menninger Perspective*, vol. 23, no. 4 (1992). (For copies, write to the Menninger Clinic, Box 829, Topeka, Kansas 66601.)

Charles, Matilda. "Grandparents as Parents." *Miami Herald*, January, 1993.

Chion-Kenney, Linda. "Advice for Grandparents." *Washington Post*, May 6, 1991.

———. "Parents of Divorce." *Washington Post*, May 6, 1991.

Cooksey, Karen. "Love Takes More Than Words." *Modern Maturity*, December 1990–January 1991.

Creighton, Linda S. "The Silent Saviors." *U.S. News and World Report*, December 16, 1991.

Edelstein, Stephanie. "Do Grandparents Have Rights?" *Modern Maturity*, December 1990–January 1991.

Fischman, Joshua. "Stepdaughter Wars/New Daddies Can't Win." *Psychology Today*, November 1988.

Goldberg, Marion Zenn. "Divorce Mediation: Panacea or Just Another Tool?" *Trial Magazine,* vol. 28, issue 9 (September 1992).

Kutner, Lawrence. "Stepfamilies Cope with New Children." *Cincinnati Enquirer,* April 23, 1989.

Mesce, Deborah. "So Long, Ozzie: 1950s-Style Family No Longer Typical." *Virginia-Pilot* (Norfolk, Virginia), March 1993.

Suchetka, Diane. "Men Dealing with Pain (Physical and Emotional)." *Ledger-Star* (Norfolk, Virginia), January 11, 1993.

NEWSLETTERS AND OTHER PUBLICATIONS

The American Family. (Collector's edition of *Life* magazine.) June 1992.

Brack, Datha Clapper, and Tirzah Schutzengel. *Grandmothers of the 1980s: An Exploratory Study of Changing Roles.* Bergen Community College, Paramus, New Jersey, n.d.

Scarsdale Family Counseling Service. "Grandparents." (A newsletter.) See especially issues no. 5 (spring 1988) and no. 9 (winter 1992).

Speak Out for Children. (Quarterly newsletter of the National Council for Children's Rights.) See vol. 6, no. 1 (winter 1990–91).

The Vital Connections: The Grandparenting Newsletter. See vol. 6 (spring 1991).

Index

Index

Index

Marriage(s)
  breakup of, 13–33
  see also Remarriage
Maternal grandparents, 76
Martindale-Hubbell Lawyers' Directory, 42
McClenahan, Carolyn, 152
McCurley, Michael, 46
Mediation, 43–48, 136, 143
  court-ordered, 134, 147
Mediation services, 41–48
Medical insurance, 56
Medicare, 56
Mensch, 11, 74, 75
Mentor role of grandparents, 3, 16–17,
  100
Minton, Dean, 96
Mirman, Denise, 48
Missing Children Help Center, 143
Mohr, Don, 45
Money management, 55, 57
Money matters, 48–57
Mortgage payments, 50, 55
Mother-daughter relationship, 123
Mother-grandmother relationship, 18
Mourning, 14–17, 23, 24–25
  see also Grief process

National Conference of Commissioners
  on Uniform State Laws, 146
National organizations, 144–45
NationsBank Corporation, 108
Neediness (adult children), 37, 86
Networking, resources for, 155–57
Neugarten, Bernice, 8
Neutrality, 72, 77
New Jersey Supreme Court, 132
Noncustodial grandparents, 77
Noncustodial parent, 2, 23, 29, 59
  and counseling, 39
  relationship with, 7–8, 79–80
Normalcy, 23, 36

Other parent, 79–80
  see also Noncustodial parent
Other side of the family, 6, 89
  building bridges with, 74–81

Overdependency
  see Dependency

Pain
  attending to, 82–83
  coping with, 88–89
  helping to ease, 16, 34–57
  and parenting, 21, 22
Parens patriae (role of state), 128, 137
Parental authority
  visitation rights and, 129–31
Parental autonomy, 123
Parenting, 5, 27
  adult children, 2
  and divorce, 14
  generational differences in, 7
Parenting skills, 21, 38, 113
Parenting style, 91
  generational differences in, 105,
  121–25
  see also Child rearing
Parents of adult children, 13–14, 16
Parents Without Partners, 41
Parent-to-parent relationship
  following divorce, 43–45
Parker, Charles, 16–17, 35, 100
Partial custody rights, 134
Perception, 99–100
Petition for visitation, 133, 135
  right to, 126–27, 128
Physical symptoms, 38
Population Reference Bureau, 153
Positive focus, 5, 17, 28, 81, 113
Post, Dianne, 46–48
Privacy (grandparents), 94, 95, 96
  loss of, 101, 114, 119
Professional help, 7, 8, 30
  finding, 40
  in mourning, 15
  see also Counseling; Therapy
Protective order, 47
Pryor, David, 146–47
Psychiatric nurses, 40

Rabinowitz, Marc, 14, 19, 23–24, 30,
  37–38, 49, 82

Index